There's So Much More

Experiencing God's Love in the Power of the Holy Spirit

By

Mary Ellen Rossman

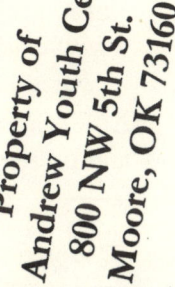

Copyright © 2003 by Mary Ellen Rossman

There's So Much More
by Mary Ellen Rossman

Printed in the United States of America

ISBN 1-594670-88-9

All rights reserved. No part of this publication may be reproduced or transmitted in any form or by any means without written permission of the author.

Excerpts from the *New American Bible* with Revised New Testament and Psalms. Copyright © 1991, 1986, 1970 Confraternity of Christian Doctrine, Inc., Washingon, DC. Used with permission. All rights reserved. No portion of the *New American Bible* may be reprinted without permission in writing from the copyright holder.

Xulon Press
www.XulonPress.com

Xulon Press books are available in bookstores everywhere, and on the Web at www.XulonPress.com.

January 17, 2004

Dear Stephen,

May the Holy Spirit fill you with "so much more" of His loving presence in your life.

God bless you!

Mary Ellen

Dedication

In gratitude to the Holy Spirit for his presence in my life - he has been my source of love even when I didn't know him, feel him, or sense him.

Thank you Holy Spirit for wanting us all to experience you more profoundly. I pray that you will use this book to reveal yourself to all those who persevere in reading it.

This is for you, dearest Holy Spirit.

Acknowledgements

I want to thank my husband Ray for his encouragement, support and for all the hours he spent reviewing this manuscript and making my job so much easier. My daughter Christine and son Raymond showed me where I needed to "tweak" it up.

I also want to thank my brothers, Edward and Thomas Farrell, my friend Cathy Lorenz and my brother-in-law Paul Weston for their advice and suggestions.

Many years ago I met two very remarkable men named Reverend Carlton French and Brother Thomas Hooper who spent approximately two years sharing with me what it meant to live as a saved, sanctified and spirit-filled Christian.

Thank you all for your patience and persistence.

Table of Contents

Preface xi
Introduction xv
  1. Gentle Stirrings of the Holy Spirit 19
  2. We Are Loved Into Love 25
  3. Who Is the Holy Spirit and What Is His
      Place in the Trinity? 31
  4. Recent Stirrings of the Holy Spirit
      in the Church 37
  5. God Really Does Love Me 43
  6. The Holy Spirit Is the Divine Love 49
  7. Baptism of Water for Repentance 55
  8. The Baptism of the Holy Spirit 67
  9. The Gift of Tongues 85
10. Baptism of Fire 99
11. Ask for More 119

Preface

One of the ways I have learned to spell the name of God is MORE. God is infinite, his love is infinite, and we have a spiritual capacity that is infinite. Every time we grow in God's love our capacity to love grows more. That is why I welcome with joy this beautiful little book that reminds me that *There's so Much More*.

The people who welcomed Jesus knew they needed more, and they saw in Jesus that *more*. People who turned a cold shoulder to Jesus were those who were satisfied with where they were. They didn't want the more Jesus had to give. And even those who said "yes" to Jesus and began to follow him soon found out he had even more to give them than they had imagined.

If you are satisfied with where you are, you don't need this book. On second thought, maybe you need it more than anybody else. It might awaken you to seek the more that you thought you didn't need. If you already yearn for more of God, then this book is like the scroll that the prophet ate. It will taste like honey and will open new horizons for you and tell you how to get there.

Mary Ellen Rossman has woven a tapestry of God's

word in Scripture with her personal experience in a way that speaks to the heart. As you read, you are likely to say, "Yes, that-or something like that-happened to me." And reading a little further you may say, "Wow, I'd really like to have what she is talking about."

When Mary Ellen asked me to look over her manuscript to check it for any theological errors, I had no idea I would offer to write a preface for it. Busy with other things, I let the manuscript sit on my desk for two months, buried under a pile of things I considered more urgent. Finally guilt overcame me and I began to read it. That's when I felt even more guilty for not reading it sooner. It challenged me to seek more of that Gift, the Holy Spirit. It will do the same for you.

I would like to comment on two points in Mary Ellen's book. The first concerns her division of the human person into *body, soul (or mind)* and *spirit.* This three-fold division, which I used in my book *Riding the Wind,* comes from Saint Paul. In 1 Thessalonians 5:23 Paul prays: "May the God of peace make you holy through and through, and may your whole being, *spirit, soul and body,* be preserved blameless for the coming of our Lord Jesus Christ." That text in turn builds on the Jewish tradition going back to the creation of the first human being, when God formed man from the earth (thus giving him a body), and then breathed into him the breath of life (the spirit) and man became a living being (or soul, Genesis 2:7).

For those of us accustomed to think of ourselves as soul and body only, this may be a bit of a surprise. After all, St. Thomas Aquinas, the church's most famous theologian, is satisfied with "soul" and "body." But even there St. Thomas distinguishes in the soul between its lower function, which is the ability to reason, and its higher function, which is contemplation, openness to the transcendent, to the infinite. That contemplative dimension corresponds to what Paul calls our *spirit.* It's the spirit in us that enables us to receive

God's spirit, the Holy Spirit, as Paul says in Romans 8:16: "The Spirit bears united witness with our spirit that we are the children of God."

Think of a tree. Its roots sink into mother earth, it's trunk gives order and shape to the life it draws from the soil, and its branches reach out like hungry arms for the sun and the rain. So too, we are brothers and sisters to the earth through our body, we "organize' life through our soul or mind, but it is our spirit that reaches out to the light and warmth of God and the refreshing rain of his Spirit. Of course, some people live their lives mostly on the bodily level, and some only on the intellectual level (I'll accept only what I can prove with my mind). But God made each of us a *capax Dei,* a capacity for God. We are whole beings only when we live on the level of the Spirit and let that life penetrate our minds and our bodies as well.

The second point I would like to address concerns the gift of tongues. Mary Ellen describes an experience where she prayed over a Chinese priest, and he understood that she was praying in Mandarin, one of the Chinese languages. She of course had no idea what she was saying, and certainly not that she was talking Mandarin. This, I believe, is an occasional "Miraculous" use of tongues, given by God when someone badly needs a sign that God is with them, as happened to be the case with this Chinese priest. This happened to me once when I was praying with a native American nun who had just learned that her father was murdered. Somehow in my prayer I used the Sioux word for "Great Spirit," and she told me later that when that happened she experienced in her spirit the resurrection of her father.

The ordinary use of tongues, however, is for one's own prayer language, a prayer of the heart or the spirit that bypasses the mental process of shaping words, and goes from the heart of the pray-er straight to the heart of God, much as a child talks to his mother before he can formulate words. It can be threatening for some people (like myself) to yield to this gift because it means letting go of control at what human beings consider the greatest mark of intelligence, acquired through years of learning: the ability to make words and sentences. It's a new experience for an adult to talk baby talk to God, but that's what the Spirit uses to get us into mystery beyond the categories of words. "Unless you become like little children..." Saint Augustine called it *jubilation*.

And it is this gift that God sometimes uses in a dramatic way to speak to the heart of others, like the Chinese priest or the Sioux nun. But don't think that you have to suddenly miraculously speak a foreign language when you yield to tongues. If you do, it's God's business, not yours. Yours is just to give your heart to God and your tongue to whatever syllables tumble out beyond words. The difficulty with tongues is not its difficulty. It's its simplicity.

But I don't want to steal any more of Mary Ellen's secrets before you find them out for yourself. Turn the page and you'll find out *there's so much more*.

Rev. George T. Montague, S. M.
Professor of Theology
St. Mary's University

Introduction

This book is written to encourage you on your life's journey to know that there is more – so much more of God's love and presence to experience, letting the Holy Spirit reveal himself to us and accepting his presence in our lives.

There was a time in my life when I wondered if there was a God. Who was he, and how could I know him? Did he really love me as I was? Or did I have to be perfect to find him? During my search, one verse of scripture that made a profound effect on me was Matthew 3:11. John the Baptist was preaching by the Jordan River, and said,

> "I am baptizing you with <u>water</u>, for <u>repentance</u>, but the one who is coming after me is mightier than I.
> I am not worthy to carry his sandals. He will baptize you with the <u>holy Spirit</u> and <u>fire</u>" (emphasis added).

Jesus and his disciples continued the baptism in water but it now brought the Holy Spirit and fire. There are 3 elements here: repentance, ministry and sanctification. Jesus was anointed in his baptism for his ministry and so are we.

A similar account is in Luke 3:16.

I believe these are specific movements of grace and do not necessarily have to be in that order. There has to be repentance and the desire to change our life. Then we need to give our life to Jesus wholeheartedly, and allow him to be Lord of our lives, represented by water baptism – which symbolizes death to the old life (going under the water) and coming alive into the new (as we come out of the water). When we are baptized with the Holy Spirit, there will be excitement in sharing the Word of God and using his gifts to minister to others as the Apostles experienced on the first Pentecost. The "fire baptism" activates our intimacy with God and holiness in us. Change takes place in us as a result of the movement of the Holy Spirit in our lives.

God works in each of us uniquely, and we all are gifted differently. We need this difference if we are to bring the good news of Jesus to a hurting world; if we are to see justice and peace reign; and if we are to understand that we are loved unconditionally by a loving God. This Baptism scripture has helped me immensely to make some sense and meaning in my life. As you read, I hope what I have written will encourage and empower you to be the man or woman God knows you can become.

This is not a theological dissertation on salvation, sanctification and in-filling of the Holy Spirit, but is written by one who had doubts and fears like most of us, who asked myself and God what life was all about, and how I fit into the big picture. I understand that many who read this may feel that when they were baptized and or confirmed, they experienced all three movements of grace. I believe that when we were baptized and confirmed we not only received the grace of the sacraments but also that we received the Holy Trinity – Father, Son, and Holy Spirit to the extent that we were open to receive this grace at that time. We began our faith journey of salvation, in-filling of the Holy Spirit and sanctification.

I also believe that this grace has to be appropriated into our lives. It is up to us to develop, explore and activate the grace of God, like the seed falling onto good ground. It needs good soil (faith-filled parents, relatives and/or good faith-filled friends), lots of water (the grace of God), plenty of sunshine (good teaching from a faith community), good nutrients (reading the Word of God). Most of all, it must be a healthy seed, which only God can produce. God himself is the faithful and patient gardener. We are all given different gifts and as we determine how to use them for the good of all, God is able to activate his grace in us by releasing us more and more in the power of his Holy Spirit.

I want to share with you what I have experienced in my life and how I feel the Holy Spirit was moving in me. This is my journey. Your experience will be different. We all release in God's grace in our own way. I pray that you will come to love, appreciate, and value this profound scripture; acquire a greater understanding of the Holy Spirit in your life; know without a shadow of a doubt how much you are loved; and be able to share God's love with others.

This book is about love – my experience of love, not my human love, but about the divine source of Love - God. As we go through life, I feel we are so busy that we seldom take time to realize that the God who created us loves us passionately and stays close to us. Because of the busyness we create we often miss the many ways God is trying to reveal his love to us. He wants so much to be allowed to move deeply in our lives and for us to be able to experience his love more profoundly. It is my desire, that you experience his love as you read this book, and begin to hunger for so much more of him.

CHAPTER ONE

Gentle Stirrings of the Holy Spirit

It was 1959 and I was sitting at my desk at the Kaupert Secretarial Institute. Kaupert's was on the third floor of the Dominican Commercial high school in Jamaica, New York - a place where Catholic girls who graduated from an academic high school and weren't going to college studied for one year to become "professional secretaries."

It was pre-Vatican II and Sister Rose Gabriel began the day as usual with a prayer. She would then tell us a joke, but this day was different. She was serious. Sister said, "You young ladies are coming into the age of the lay apostolate." We didn't have a clue to what she was talking about and she could see it written all over our faces. "Lay apostolate?" we asked. "Yes, the time is coming when the work of the Catholic church will more and more be in the hands of lay people" she replied. We were dead silent. We liked it the way it was. Let the nuns, priests, and brothers be the professionals. We'd do our thing and they could do theirs. "You will see the day when the message of Jesus will be told and taught by ordinary people. You will be required to take on more responsibility for sharing your faith with the coming generations," she continued. Sister Rose Gabriel was prophesying ahead of her time.

The Coming of Vatican II

With the 1960's came the second Vatican Council of the Catholic Church. People began to question authority - social, political, and even ecclesiastical. Pop culture heroes such as the Beatles were quoting their gurus. All hell was breaking loose in the United States over the morality of the Vietnam conflict, drugs were rampant and we were in the midst of the sexual revolution. Time magazine published an issue questioning if there really was a God. Today it's more than forty years later and Sister Rose Gabriel's prophecy has come true. How did she know?

There were rumblings in the church at that time. The new pope (John XXIII) was calling the people to open wide the doors and windows of the church to let the Holy Spirit move. Bishops, cardinals, priests, brothers, sisters, and lay people from all around the world came to Rome to re-evaluate church teachings at the Council. Drastic changes were made in the liturgy, and penitential rites. Catholics were told to be more ecumenical. Spirituality as well as many religious observances, was being challenged. This brought chaos and confusion to many in the church. Some people whose only connections with the church were the traditional rituals, rules and regulations were devastated. "What has become of our church?" they asked. I too had my questions. At eighteen years of age I wondered if the church was the biggest scam going. Being that I came from a large Irish Catholic family with an aunt who was a Dominican nun, a brother studying to become a Maryknoll missionary, and a cousin in a Jesuit seminary, I knew enough to keep my doubts to myself. What would they think if I questioned the authority of the church?

I actually thought about being a nun while in elementary and high school. I remember in 8th grade, Fr. McMullen, our local parish priest, came into our classroom and asked us to think about what we wanted to do with the rest of our lives. He said to ask God to show us what his will was for us, and to pray to the Holy Spirit for grace to live it to the best of our ability. He said, "When you are in the will of God you have peace." So from the days of 8th grade I prayed every day to know the will of God. "Do you want me to marry? If so, please help me find the most perfect man on earth." "Do you want me to be a nun? If so, please show me what kind of a nun (Dominican, Franciscan, Josephite)." "Do you want me to remain single? Please keep me chaste and pure."

I think it was my senior year at St. Agnes Academic high school, when I was daydreaming in class, that I pictured myself in a convent dressed in a nun's habit going to the side door of the convent to bring in the bottles of milk. I saw myself grabbing the milkman and bringing him into the convent and then I knew... I could never become a nun! However, I continued to pray to the Holy Spirit while I went to business school and until I married.

Upon graduating from Kaupert's, I commuted by train from East Rockaway on Long Island, to New York City to work as an executive secretary in a large advertising agency on Madison Avenue. I loved my job and the people I worked with. For a while, I experienced culture shock. Up until this period of my life, I had always been surrounded by Catholics - Catholic elementary school, Catholic high school, and Catholic business school.

The people at work lived such different lives. None of my new friends had ever read the lives of the great men and women in the church. One of my friends accompanied me to daily Mass on our lunch hour. I remember we carried our new "Daily Missals." We were quite modern. Our missals were in Latin – and English!

The Holy Spirit Has Been Moving Through the Years

Around this time in history, our government developed the Peace Corps where young men and women volunteered their service to developing countries, for approximately two years, to share technology, farming methods, and education. There were some good things that came out of the 1960's and one of them was an awareness of our responsibility to love and share with others.

I had already been exposed to this through both my parents. For many years my mother used to send care packages of toothpaste, toothbrushes, soap, etc. to a missionary priest in the Philippines. I remember my father's concern for others and wanting us to consider others when he collected money from us all to send money to the missionary priests supported by the Propagation of the Faith. During the Lenten season we had little Lenten boxes from school where we saved our candy money from the treats that we didn't eat during Lent and the money was sent to the needy. I believe these were the first stirrings of the Holy Spirit before Vatican II in our family.

As we grew older, my brother Tom joined the Extension Lay Volunteers. He had a master's degree in education and went to work as a principal in a segregated African-American school in Mansura, Louisiana. When the schools became integrated he went to work in Jackson, Michigan to set up a youth and employment center for inner city children and their families.

In 1964 I went with my husband, Ray, when he was stationed in Catania, Italy at a Naval Air station. Since it was a temporary 6 months assignment there was no housing on the base so I lived in the city. I looked for a way to spend my free time and spoke to the military Catholic Chaplain. He

There's So Much More

put me in touch with an order of nuns who went to the homes of hospitalized poor women and who did the women's daily chores while they were recuperating. Even though the sisters did not speak English and I did not speak Italian we managed to communicate. I was 24 years old at the time so I had a lot of strength and energy. In the morning I would walk several miles from my apartment to the convent where I met the nuns. From there we would set out on foot to the families who needed help washing clothes, cooking, feeding the children, and cleaning their houses. I studied Spanish and Latin in high school so I felt confident that if I didn't know a word in Italian I would blurt out a word or two in Latin or Spanish and sure enough they understood me. I never left home without my Italian dictionary. I loved being with the nuns and working with them. They had generous and good hearts. When we returned to the states, I taught catechism to fourth and fifth graders.

I feel the Holy Spirit moves us to activity – the kind that helps mankind. I had always loved the Holy Spirit, had devotion to him and tried to be sensitive to him, but somehow or other I still felt there had to be more to our Catholic faith than just doing good for others. I know he uses our feeble attempts for good. However, I still had a lot to learn about the movement of the Holy Spirit and how he wants us to come to him, to allow him to be in charge. Sometimes our motives for helping others are to achieve self-acclaim. Before I would think of ways to please him - now I ask him what he wants and then pray that he would empower me to work with him as he brings about his will in my life and the lives of others.

The decade of the 1960's was a strange time in the history of our country, and our church. Catholics were encouraged to reach out and love others, to share and to care, while at the same time the hippies were also talking about love and peace. During the 1960's we were in the anguish of the Vietnam conflict. People questioned our purpose and motives for being in Vietnam. There were factions on both sides. The hippies spoke about love and peace, while all around us was chaos and confusion. I witnessed a country torn apart on every side by people talking about love, yet destroying themselves by drug induced orgies, winding up in an insane asylum or dead before the age of 25. What was happening to our country? What was love really all about?

CHAPTER TWO

We Are Loved Into Love

My most powerful encounter with the source of all love began in March 1972. I had been feeling an emptiness in my soul even though I had everything a young woman could ask for – a wonderful husband; 4 healthy children; a lovely home on Long Island, New York; and the ability to travel the world over. Even with all this, something was still gnawing at me.

Having been born and raised a Catholic, I followed all the rules and regulations. I had been a daily communicant and read the lives of the saints, yet there was a stirring in my soul that I couldn't ignore. I felt I was missing something – something that I knew was a yearning in my soul to know God more intimately.

Then one day I read in our parish bulletin that there was going to be a square dance for married couples and they needed volunteers to meet on a certain day to help organize it. It was at this meeting that I met Rosemary, a young woman who shared something with me that was going to change my life forever. She told me that after Vatican II there was a strong movement of the Holy Spirit in the Catholic Church. I told her that the Holy Spirit was an old friend of mine, since I had received the sacrament of Confirmation in elementary school. I prayed to the Holy Spirit for wisdom when I had exams. As an executive secretary in New York City I prayed to the Holy Spirit before I answered the phone that I would give the correct information to each caller. I said novenas to the Holy Spirit, and I prayed to the Holy Spirit for a good husband. Prayer to the Holy Spirit was already a part of my life.

She said it was bigger than just asking the Holy Sprit for help. It was coming together as a Christian community to praise and worship "in the Holy Spirit" using the gifts of the Holy Spirit just as the early Christians did. I said that would be nice, but nobody I knew had these gifts; such as tongues, interpretation of tongues, healing, miracles, words of wisdom, knowledge, understanding, or discernment of spirits. They were given to the first apostles and disciples to build up the early church. She challenged me and said, "Don't you think the church needs them now?" "Well, yes I guess," I responded, "but how do you meet people like that?" I invited her over for lunch and she explained to me that praying for something you want is not the same as worshipping, adoring, praising and thanking God. I asked her if I could go with her to one of these "Christian communities" and she said only after I read, "Catholic Pentecostals" by Kevin and Dorothy Ranaghan and "The Cross and the Switchblade" by Rev. David Wilkerson. Within a short time I had finished reading both books, so I telephoned her again and asked if I could go with her to the next meeting. She agreed to take me.

When we arrived at the leader's home I was warmly welcomed by Sonia and Jack Fischer and joined about 20 to 30 men, women and children in their family room sitting in chairs and on the floor in a large circle around the room. There were inspirational posters on the wall as well as other decorations. Someone started playing a guitar and led the group in songs of praise, worship and adoration. I joined in the singing and began to relax. Keeping my eyes open, I watched the others as they sang wholeheartedly. Some people were raising their hands, some clapping, and others just singing quietly. Some had their eyes open and some were closed. Everyone was very respectful and they seemed to believe that Jesus was really present in the room as they worshipped him. They said, "Where two or more are gathered in his Name, he would be there," and "God inhabits the praise of his people." After the praise they began singing in strange languages, followed by silence for a few minutes. Everyone sat still and waited for someone to interpret the tongues. As I remember, it was a message of encouragement and love. Then some people began to share scriptures that had a special meaning for them and told how the Lord was working in their lives during the week. This was followed by prayer and intercession for each other and then a final hymn. Some people asked for specific prayers while others prayed over them as they sat in their chair. The rest of the people went into the kitchen for coffee and fellowship.

On the way home from the meeting I thought about the people I had just met. Not one of them asked me what my husband did for a living, who my parents were, did I have a college education, what part of town I lived in or what kind of car I drove. My husband had been in the military for 6 years and everyone knew if your husband was an officer or an enlisted person. I always felt I was being categorized by rank and I never felt loved and respected for myself as a person. This meeting was the first time that I felt loved and accepted by perfect strangers. These people seemed to have a different kind of love and I wanted to learn how they came by it. I felt that I could have been a prostitute or a drug addict and they would have loved me the same. The following week while visiting my brothers and sisters, I caught myself saying to them, "Do we really realize how much God loves us?" "I can't believe how much God loves us," "Do you feel God's love for you?" and similar sentences. For some reason or other, I began to experience the loving presence of God, for a solid week after being with this "Christian community," for only two hours.

Love Changes You

Since that first prayer meeting, Holy Scripture has come alive, a new joy has filled my countenance and I experience more intimacy with God. These changes in my life are the effects of the Baptism of the Holy Spirit that John the Baptist prophesied and Jesus promised to his followers. I have come to love and respect myself, and to love and respect others, in a healthy way. I discovered that there is a big difference between human love and divine love. I know when I run out of human love I can depend on the divine love to pull me through. I always felt there had to be a way to love beyond myself, but nobody could tell me how to reach it. I had to experience God's love to understand – and you can too. The secret is in having an open mind and heart to receive the divine love.

I've learned that God truly inhabits the praise of his people. As St. Paul writes in 1 Corinthians 12, 13, and 14, the Holy Spirit has so many wonderful gifts for all of us – and the greatest of these is love – His love for us, and through us, reaching out to others.

In the book, "Welcoming the New Millennium, Wisdom from Pope John Paul II," (The Word Among Us Press, Ijamsville, MD, copyright 1999) in chapter 7 it says,

> "Man cannot live without love. He remains a being that is incomprehensible for himself, his life is senseless, if love is not revealed to him, if he does not encounter love, if he does not experience it and make it his own, if he does not participate

intimately in it. This, as has already been said, is why Christ the Redeemer 'fully reveals man to himself.' If we may use the expression, this is the human dimension of the mystery of the redemption. In this dimension man finds again the greatness, dignity and value that belong to his humanity. In the mystery of the redemption man becomes newly 'expressed' and, in a way, is newly created. He is newly created! 'There is neither Jew nor Greek, there is neither slave nor free, there is neither male nor female; for you are all one in Christ.'"
(Galatians 3:28).

This is why I believe that we must find God's love. We need to look around and see the many ways that God loves us each day. We can do this by making it a habit to thank God for all the wonderful things he has done for us in our lives. God told the Israelites to continue to remember every day the wonders he did for them. If you feel that you have never experienced God's love for you, I want to encourage you to make a promise to yourself that for one week you will be continually on the lookout for his love. Train yourself to be alert and to ask God to reveal his love to you. Then acknowledge it when you see it, by saying "thank you" to God.

It has been 30 years since I first began to realize how much God loves me. Through the years of "walking in the Spirit" I have come to appreciate the movement of the Holy Spirit in my life. For it is the Holy Spirit who continually reveals his presence of love in our lives. He wants to help us understand that Jesus really is Lord of our lives. Because out of Jesus' tremendous love for us, he gave up his own life that we may come to know the love of our heavenly Father.

CHAPTER THREE

Who Is the Holy Spirit and What Is His Place In the Trinity?

Our Catholic catechism teaches us that the Holy Spirit is the third person of the Blessed Trinity and I feel he is the most misunderstood. There is only one God, yet three divine persons. We can picture the creator of the universe, our heavenly Father, in long white robes and white hair as depicted by Michaelangelo in the Sistine chapel in Rome. We can visualize Jesus as a Jewish man with long dark hair and beard and sandals on his feet. But the Holy Spirit is mysterious to most of us. Artists have usually portrayed him as a white dove, representing the peace one feels in his presence. Sometimes he is represented by fire symbolizing his enormous sanctifying power. We know he is present to us but we can't imagine him. We cannot see him in our mind's eye.

When I am outside and see the breeze moving through the leaves on the tree or the fog rolling over the fields, I think of the Holy Spirit. I might not be able to see air, but when it moves through the leaves on a windy day or is filled with moisture on a foggy day, I can grasp the reality of his presence. Although I cannot see air tangibly, I can feel its effect. The Holy Spirit is more powerful than a tornado and yet so gentle and still as a day on the beach with no breeze. How awesome and powerful he is, yet so still and gentle. It is the movement and power of the Holy Spirit in our life that accomplishes all good and empowers us to love beyond what we are really capable of.

The Place of the Holy Spirit in the Trinity

I picture the Holy Spirit as an enormous movement of divine love moving from the Father to the Son. The Divine Love moving from the Lover to the Beloved and the Beloved receiving this love and returning it back to the Lover. The Holy Spirit, is the Divine Love and third person of the Blessed Trinity who moves from the Father to Jesus and from Jesus to the Father. It is the Holy Spirit, the Divine Love, who wants to draw us into this union between the Father and the Son. This is his ministry. He is the matchmaker for our heavenly Father who is seeking a bride for his Son Jesus.

In Old Testament times, when Abraham saw that it was time for his son Isaac to marry, he called his chief administrator and asked him to find a suitable bride for Isaac. Notice it was the father, who decided when it was time for Isaac to marry. The chief administrator knew Isaac since he was a child and knew his temperament and everything about him. It was the chief administrator, Abraham's matchmaker, who chose Rebecca for Isaac and when Isaac saw Rebecca for the first time, he was thrilled that she was the one chosen for him.

So too, with the Holy Spirit. He is the matchmaker for the Father, who is constantly looking for the bride of Jesus. And it is the Holy Spirit who will draw us into this union with the bridegroom (Jesus) when it is the proper time. If we want more than anything to be the "Bride," we should be on good terms with the Holy Spirit. I believe the Holy Spirit is the one who not only picks and chooses who will become the bride, but he also prepares her (makes her holy and sanctified), since he is a holy God and cannot have anyone in his presence who is not holy. When Jesus, the bridegroom comes for his bride, I want to be ready and waiting with the Holy Spirit. Revelation 22:17,20 says,

> "The Spirit and the bride (hopefully us) say, 'Come.'....
> The one who gives this testimony (Jesus) says, 'Yes, I am coming soon.' Amen! Come, Lord Jesus!"

This shows we should be on the alert, watching and waiting with the Holy Spirit for the arrival of Jesus, and the wedding banquet. When the wedding occurs, I do not want to be a bridesmaid, or a guest at the wedding, – I want to be the bride!

Matthew 25:1-13 tells the parable of the ten virgins – 5 foolish and 5 wise. The foolish ones were not prepared for the bridegroom because they didn't bring extra flasks of oil for their lamps to hold them through the night and had to leave to see if they could find some at that very late hour. The 5 wise virgins brought enough for the night and when the bridegroom arrived they were ready and walked right in with him. The foolish ones never arrived on time and were left outside. Jesus was warning us to be ready with our lamps burning and plenty of oil in reserve so that when he comes to claim his bride we are ready. The Holy Spirit will see to it that we have plenty of that oil.

The Holy Spirit Unites Us

On the night of the Last Supper, Jesus prayed,

> "I pray not only for them, but also for those who will believe in me through their word, so that they may all be one, as you, Father, are in me and I in you, that they also may be in us, that the world may believe that you sent me. And I have given them the glory you gave me, so that they may be one, as we are one, I in them and you in me, that they may be brought to perfection as one, that the world may know that you sent me, and that you loved them even as you loved me."
>
> (John 17:20-23)

This is Jesus praying that we may experience our heavenly Father's love as he experiences it. Jesus is one in the Father and was praying that we could be one in them. I believe it is the mission of the Holy Spirit to draw us into this union. It is God's desire to share his love with his children and that is why he sent Jesus into this world.

In John 14: 16,17 Jesus was speaking to his disciples when he said,

> "I will ask the Father, and he will give you another Advocate to be with you always, the Spirit of truth, which the world cannot accept, because it neither sees nor knows it. But you know it, because it remains with you, and will be in you."

Notice Jesus said the world at large cannot receive him, for it isn't looking for him and doesn't recognize him. Jesus was telling his disciples that the Holy Spirit comes only to those who really want him residing inside them. The Holy Spirit will come only where he is wanted. Are we looking for him? Do we really want him in our lives? Do we recognize him when he is moving in our lives? Have we invited the Holy Spirit to reside or release in us for all eternity? In

There's So Much More

1 John 4:13, Scripture tells us that,

> "This is how we know that we remain in him (the Father) and he in us, that he has given us of his Spirit."

We need the Holy Spirit just as the first Apostles and disciples did. Jesus commanded them to go back to Jerusalem and wait for the Holy Spirit, because he knew that they needed to be one in him just as Jesus was one in the Father, and only the Holy Spirit could draw us into this union.

In John 15:26, Jesus reminds his disciples,

> "When the Advocate comes whom I will send you from the Father, the Spirit of truth that proceeds from the Father, he will testify to me."

This shows that the Holy Spirit comes from the Father to witness to Jesus and reveal that Jesus was sent from the Father.

And again in John 16:13 at the Last Supper Jesus told his apostles,

> "But when he comes, the Spirit of truth, he will guide you to all truth. He will not speak on his own, but he will speak what he hears, and will declare to you the things that are coming."

Jesus was giving us his greatest gift – The Holy Spirit. He reminded the apostles that it would be the Holy Spirit who had the power to keep them going, to be their love when they were afraid, to be their wisdom when they didn't know what to do, to empower them when they had no courage. We are all invited to receive this divine gift of the Holy Spirit. All we have to say is, "Yes, I want more of you

Holy Spirit" and really mean it.

The Holy Spirit Is the Power to Love

I had prayed earnestly to be able to love more. I wanted to love God, my husband, my children, my parents, my friends to the best of my ability. It wasn't until around the age of 31 that I finally found out that I could love only so far, and that I needed the love that only the Holy Spirit could give. There is a big difference between human love and divine love. And only the Holy Spirit (who is the divine love) can love through us to reach out to those we are having difficulty loving.

The leaders of Vatican II prayed earnestly for the Holy Spirit to be poured out on the church anew, so let's take a look back and see how the Holy Spirit has been moving in this century.

CHAPTER FOUR

Recent Stirrings of the Holy Spirit in the Church

In the last years of the nineteenth century, Sister Elena Guerra, foundress of the Oblate Sisters of the Holy Spirit in Cucca, Italy, sent 12 confidential letters to Pope Leo XIII urging him to renew the church through devotion to the Holy Spirit. His response was to publish the encyclical, <u>Divinum Illud Munus</u>, which was distributed to all countries around the world. Unfortunately, most Catholics did not read the encyclical, or paid little attention to it. On behalf of the church, Pope Leo XIII began the 20th century by dedicating it to the Holy Spirit.

Some people however took this message seriously. I can remember in elementary and high school reciting a prayer to the Holy Spirit. It went something like this, "Come Holy Spirit. Fill the hearts of your faithful. Enkindle in them the fire of your love. Send forth your Spirit, and we will be created, and you will renew the face of the earth." Sister William Eugene, a Dominican nun who was a friend of my family taught us a novena to the Holy Spirit in the 1940's and 1950's. I remember saying it several times. So there was some teaching on the Holy Spirit, but it was mostly asking the Holy Spirit for something.

Within a short period of time after the publication of <u>Divinum Illud Munus</u>, some people who were praying to the Holy Spirit for his anointing, were filled to overflowing with the power of a new Pentecost. When they shared this great grace with their congregation, many did not understand the importance of what was happening. This did not stop the Holy Spirit. As these Christians shared this powerful experience with others their numbers increased rapidly and they were soon called Pentecostals. They were experiencing the power of the Holy Spirit exactly as the first apostles and disciples did on Pentecost.

Before convening the Second Vatican Council in 1959, Pope John XXIII also prayed for a new Pentecost and asked God to open wide the windows and doors of the Catholic Church to the Holy Spirit. His prayer was, "Renew your wonders in our time, as though for a new Pentecost."

In 1967, a handful of students and professors from Duquesne University and Notre Dame University came together at a retreat house (The Ark and the Dove) in Pittsburgh, Pennsylvania. Some of them were already involved in Bible studies and the Catholic Cursillo movement. They met with some people from other denominations who had already experienced the Pentecostal phenomenon. Together they humbly prayed that the Holy Spirit would pour out his power on them as in a new Pentecost. They were blessed to overflowing with the loving and powerful presence of the Holy Spirit and the release of his ministerial gifts. When they went back to school they shared this great blessing with their fellow students and professors, and they too, began to release in the Holy Spirit. What began at Duquesne University quickly spread to Notre Dame, and the University of Michigan.

This was the beginning of the outpouring of the ministerial gifts, sometimes called charisms, of the Holy Spirit that

St. Paul describes in 1 Corinthians 12 in such abundance to the church. Since 1967 this movement of the Holy Spirit known as the Catholic Charismatic Renewal has spread worldwide and the Catholic Church is now experiencing the answer to the prayers of Pope Leo XIII and Pope John XXIII for a new Pentecost.

The Holy Spirit has been present and moving in the heart of the church since the first century, and especially in the lives of the saints. The early doctors of the church, such as Tertullian (c.160-c.225), Cyril of Jerusalem (c.315-387), Basil of Caesarea (c.330-379), and John Chrysostom (c.347-407), to name only a few, have all mentioned in their sermons and writings the importance of seeing the gifts of the Holy Spirit manifested in the lives of the newly baptized. The Holy Spirit has been alive and active throughout the centuries in the lives of the saints. Now God is doing an awesome work in the world today thanks to the prayers of these two Popes, and the faithfulness and obedience of those few Catholic students and professors.

God is pouring out His Spirit upon all mankind and giving us gifts as he prophesied in Joel 3: 1-2, saying,

> "Then afterward I will pour out
> my spirit upon all mankind.
> Your sons and daughters shall prophesy,
> your old men shall dream dreams,
> your young men shall see visions;
> Even upon the servants and the handmaids,
> in those days, I will pour out my spirit."

He is pouring out his ministerial gifts of the Holy Spirit. These gifts are very powerful and very real, and are used to build up the body of Christ. All the gifts, such as prophecy, a word of wisdom, a word of knowledge, a word of understanding, healing, miracles, tongues, interpretation of tongues and discernment of spirits are needed by our church in order to combat the forces of evil in our society today. They are extremely powerful tools to accomplish the work Jesus commissioned us to do.

Fr. George Montague, and Fr. Kilian McDonnell co-authors of a booklet called, "Fanning the Flame," (The Liturgical Press, Collegeville, MN, copyright 1991) on page 12 say,

> "Fuller life in the Holy Spirit, the Spirit's charismatic anointing, endows the church with a full range of gifts. Gifts of adoration, praise, and prayer deepen the contemplative dimension of Christian faith. Gifts of service animate a life of Christian holiness committed to justice. All the charisms bring a new docility to the Spirit, an expectant faith in God's saving intervention in human affairs, an enhanced zeal for the gospel, and a respect for authority in the church."

They conclude on page 27 saying,

> "All are called to fan into flame the gift of the Holy Spirit received in the sacraments of initiation. God freely gives this grace, but it requires a personal response of ongoing conversion to the Lordship of Jesus Christ and openness to the transforming presence and power of the Holy Spirit. Only in the Holy Spirit will the church be able to respond to its pastoral needs and those of the world."

Our church has been extremely blessed throughout our history going back from earliest times to the present with the presence of the Holy Spirit. However I believe that the Holy Spirit and the gifts and graces from our sacraments of initiation must be embraced, encountered, and appropriated if we are to regenerate the lives of our church members. We have a treasure in the Holy Spirit and in our history of his movement in the Catholic Church. I pray that we will everyday invite the Holy Spirit to be more active and that we will see his movement becoming more and more powerful in our lives each day. The Holy Spirit has so much more of his life for us, but we must ask for it. Let us pray daily, "Come Holy Spirit, I need you. Come Holy Spirit I want you. Come Holy Spirit I love you." And then look for the ways he is moving in your life, recognize his love for you and share it with others.

CHAPTER FIVE

God Really Does Love Me

I believe the reason our heavenly father sent Jesus into the world was to reveal his fatherly love. God the father loved us so much and saw what a mess we were making with what he had given us, that he knew he had to send Jesus into our world to show us, by example, how he expected us to live. First he sent his prophets to us throughout the ages, and what did we do to them? We persecuted them and, finally, murdered most of them. Our heavenly Father knew how risky it would be to send Jesus, but he loved us so much that he was willing to go to the nth degree to bring all of us to himself, even at the cost of an excruciatingly painful death of his most beloved son. What love he has for you and me!

In 1 John 4:9, 10 it says,

> "In this way the love of God was revealed to us: God sent his only Son into the world so that we might have life through him. In this is love: not that we have loved God, but that he loved us and sent his Son as expiation for our sins."

This scripture is one of the most powerful statements of

God's love for us. We could pray over it for years but never realize the full mystery of this scripture. For thirty years of my life, I had an intellectual knowledge of this scripture, but when it came down to applying this to my life I was left empty-handed. I remember crying out to God saying, "God are you out there? Don't you care about me? Are you real? Can you hear me? If you are out there I need to know or I won't believe in you anymore! This is it! You have one last chance! Please, I need you!"

I was a daily communicant, born and raised a Catholic, following the letter of the law, teaching religious education, and I was crying out to God asking him if he was real. All my life I thought I had an understanding of who he was, and yet I had never met him or understood that God loved me first. I kept him at arms-length so that I could be in control of my life – living the way I wanted and then telling him what I wanted and needed and expecting him to jump when I called.

However, within a short period of time, after calling out to him, several events began to unfold that helped me know without a shadow of a doubt that God was very real. He revealed to me that he loved me with an unfathomable love. He wanted nothing more from me than for me to allow him to love me. Yes, that's right, he just wanted to love me — nothing more, nothing less. I didn't have to be or do anything to make him love me. Jesus did it all for me on Calvary.

One morning shortly after I had cried out to God to prove to me if he were real, I woke up with a thought running through my head. "Go and see Father Judge. Go and see Father Judge." Ray, my husband, was a pilot with Pan Am and was on a flight. As I changed the babies' diapers and fed them their breakfast, the same thought kept coming. "Go and see Father Judge."

How could I go anywhere? I was at home on a weekday with 4 small children and where could I get a baby-sitter?

Then I remembered it was a school holiday. By 11:00 A.M., I still couldn't get the thought out of my head. So I called Father Judge.

Father Judge was a priest in the parish I grew up in. "Where was he now?" I thought. The last that I had heard he had been stationed at a parish not too far from the town that I now lived in. I looked up the number in the phone book and dialed his number. Surprisingly he answered. "Hello?" "Uh, Father Judge? This is Mary Ellen Farrell Rossman. I don't know if you remember me, but I went to St. Raymond's elementary school twenty years ago." "Oh, yes Mary Ellen, I remember you. How are you?" he said. Oh no! He remembered me. "Well Father, I thought I might come over to see you some time," I mumbled. "You are most welcome, Mary Ellen, when can you come?" he said. I decided to meet him that very day.

When I arrived at his office, he gave me a warm greeting and sat back in his chair while I ranted and raved about why I was leaving the Catholic Church. I told him, that every Sunday I listened to sermons about loving your neighbor as yourself. "But they never tell you how!" He patiently listened for quite some time, and then shared some of his thoughts and feelings. I don't remember any of his words, but the effect on me completely changed my life.

Even now I will never forget the feeling I had standing outside my car after our visit, looking up to heaven and saying out loud, "You are not way out there! You are right here with me now, aren't you?" As I drove home God's peace and joy filled my heart. That evening Ray arrived home and when I told him what I had done, he too experienced the same peace and joy. What was it in this humble priest that changed me? As I look back thirty years later, I know that Fr. Judge was filled with the power of the Holy Spirit and his divine love. He never judged or condemned me as I questioned everything I had been taught. He loved me right where I was.

The presence of the Holy Spirit was so strong in him that it leaked out of him and quenched my thirsting soul, and refreshed me like a gentle rain. I actually felt like a gentle rain of love was all around me and that I had been in a desert. This rain was quenching my thirst and reviving my spirit. Just coming into the presence of this gentle man, who was so filled with the power of the Holy Spirit, was like drinking living water and giving me new life.

Now I understood what Jesus meant in John 4:14, when he told the Samaritan woman,

> "But whoever drinks the water I shall give will never thirst; the water I shall give will become in him a spring of water welling up to eternal life."

Up until this time in my life I had been self-righteously satisfied and believed that if I just did enough good things and did only a few bad things I would win eternal life. I was only beginning to learn that God's ways are completely different than ours.

Jesus also told the Samaritan woman in verse 23 and 24 of the same chapter,

> "But the hour is coming, and is now here, when true worshipers will worship the Father in Spirit and truth; and indeed the Father seeks such people to worship him. God is Spirit, and those who worship him must worship in Spirit and truth."

God had been waiting for me to know my need of him for so long. I never realized he waits for an invitation and loves us so passionately that he really wants to be more intimately involved in our lives. This was one of the first encounters of coming to the understanding that God truly loves me and is so gentle and kind. He initiates the relationship by allowing us to see our real need for him and then ever so gently reveals the many ways he loves us.

It was shortly thereafter that I met the woman in my parish who told me about the Holy Spirit and the charismatic prayer meetings.

CHAPTER SIX

The Holy Spirit Is the Divine Love

I started going to charismatic prayer meetings March 16, 1972 and several months later, on the first weekend of June (which was Pentecost weekend), I had an opportunity to go with some friends to a charismatic conference at Notre Dame University in Indiana.

One of the speakers told us about the Divine Love living in us. This Divine Love goes far beyond human love and that Jesus wants us to ask for it. When I observed the 50,000 attendees I knew there was something different about them. They were kind and considerate to each other while waiting on line for meals and for entrance to the stadium. They seemed to be filled with a joy and peace that was catching. I could actually see and feel the different kind of love they possessed, and I wanted it. I prayed to God saying, "Lord, my husband is home caring for 4 small children for 4 days, and it was a big sacrifice to come here. I would like to ask you for a gift this weekend. I would like to have this kind of love."

The next speaker reminded us of the scripture in Matthew 5:23-24, which read,

> "Therefore, if you bring your gift to the altar, and there recall that your brother has anything against you, leave your gift there at the altar, go first and be reconciled with your brother, and then come and offer your gift."

She said if you want anything from God, be sure before you approach the altar of God to first go and forgive all those who have hurt you throughout your life. She told about a healing that took place in her life when she was diagnosed with a tumor the size of a grapefruit in her abdomen area and she prayed often for God to heal her. When her doctor told her the tumor was getting too large and that she could wait no longer she submitted and entered the hospital. The night before her operation a few people from her parish came over to visit and prayed for her. After they left, she remembered someone who had hurt her and decided to forgive her and wrote her a note. When she did this she felt a sense of peace and went to sleep. The next morning she placed her hand on her abdomen and could not feel the tumor. When the orderly entered her room with the gurney she asked the man to wait and she called the doctor. Upon examination he could not find the tumor and called in another doctor to examine her also. She was released from the hospital and never had the problem again. She told us that she believed if we want anything from God, first take care of all our relationships with others and then come to him with our needs.

I knew I wanted to possess this Divine Love more than anything else in the world, so I began to ask myself who were the people in my life that hurt me? I prayed and asked God to reveal anyone that I was holding a grudge against. Beginning in the early stages of my life, I went through every instance of reproach I could remember. Before I knew it people came into my mind and as I presented them to God I asked him to forgive the person; that I forgave the person;

and asked God to forgive me for holding on to the grudge for so long.

I also had to look at all the people I wounded by my impatience, my jealousy, being insensitive in my thoughts, words, or actions and asked God to forgive me also.

It was 1972 and the theme of the conference for that year was "Jesus is Lord!" As I looked around the stadium I could see cardinals, bishops, priests and lay men and women of every age group, race and nationality processing into the stadium. It was an awesome sight! I will never forget the sound of the music and the wholehearted praise, worship and adoration that filled the stadium. While I joined in the singing I caught sight of the banners on either end of the stadium which stated that, "Jesus is Lord!"

I began to think about the cover page of a recent edition of Time Magazine which read, "Is God Dead?" and about all the turmoil of the 1960's and early 1970's. What did I believe? Did I really believe that Jesus is Lord? Had I made an adult commitment to allow Jesus to be Lord of my life? What would that entail to surrender my life, my husband, children, friends and hopes and dreams for the future?

In the past, my parents made that commitment for me at Baptism, and as a young teenager with the knowledge I had, I made that commitment at Confirmation. But now at 31 years of age would I allow Jesus to be Lord of my life – surrendering everyone and everything I loved over to Jesus? As I pondered these questions, I realized that God was waiting for me to make a decision – Jesus as Lord of my life or Mary Ellen trying to be Lord?

I wanted this Divine Love more than anything in the world, and so I made a promise to God. "From this day forward, I choose and will forever acknowledge you, Jesus Christ as my Lord and Savior. I invite you, Divine Love, to come into me and I give myself to you and choose to let you be in charge of my life, my husband, my children, my hopes and my dreams."

Earlier I said that God inhabits the praise of his people, and that there were thousands of people praising God. As I made this profession of faith, the presence of God became so strong that I felt that I would faint.

For some time, I experienced his enormous loving presence. I felt that I was connected to God through my spirit and that my mind and body were temporally suspended from thinking, feeling or expressing themselves. I don't know exactly how long this feeling of unity with God lasted, but all of a sudden I started thinking, "Oh, this is way too powerful for me, I could suffocate and die, for this love is so enormous and so strong." At that moment I realized how our soul (intellect, willpower, emotions) and our body are so different from our spirit. I sensed God's presence so intensely for some time in my spirit. He was so enormous, so bright, and loved me so passionately. Yet it was my mind and body that made it difficult for me to tolerate the presence of this holy God. When I allowed my mind to start feeling and thinking again I began to fear that I would suffocate from pure joy at his loving presence. I remember from my old catechism book the question about, "What is heaven?" The answer was, "Heaven is the presence of the Beatific Vision." If what I had experienced was the Beatific Vision, I knew I wanted to spend all eternity in his presence.

I had no idea God was so huge and his love so overwhelming. He was full of love and light and wanted so much to love me that I thought I would die. It was the greatest outpouring of love I have ever experienced in my life and I know without a shadow of a doubt that our God is full of love for us. His love is far bigger than his universe and his love exceeds his creation. It is mind-boggling. It has been 30 years now and I can still remember how bright and loving and powerful he is.

I have never regretted surrendering my life to him. Jesus

has been faithful to all his promises and surrounded me with many blessings. I wish I could say the same for myself toward him, but whenever I fall I confess my sin and know that he has forgiven me, and still loves and cares for me. I want to thank him a million times over for what he did for me on Calvary because now I understand that it was my sin that was washed clean by his blood two thousand years ago. I know that there is a big difference between human love and divine love. We as humans can only love so far, but with the power of the Holy Spirit (who is the Divine Love) living in us we can love beyond what we could ever hope for. We can be receptacles of his love, as Fr. Judge was for me. When we need more love the Divine Love living in us can move in and through us to others if we let him.

The Divine Love Empowers Us

Shortly after this charismatic conference, I visited my sister's best friend, Mary (who was also her sister-in-law). She was only 30 years old and was in the hospital dying from cancer. She had only a few days to live. I lived out of town at the time and remember walking apprehensively down the corridor to her room. I began to pray. "Lord, I don't know what to say to her. I'm bringing her flowers so she can enjoy them now. But Lord I have nothing else to give her. Jesus I know you live inside me, and as I walk into her room I know you will come in with me. I don't want to say or do anything stupid so I'm asking you to come in the room with me and sit down beside her. Please Lord would you stay there with her and fill her with your love and your presence, so when she dies she will be caught up into your glory."

I entered her room, and was greeted by her parents. We talked, we laughed, and we cried. I said good-bye to Mary and gave her a big hug. I flew back home the next day and she died a few days later. A year later I returned to New

York, and while visiting my sister Peggy, I was told that her mother and father-in-law were coming over. When they arrived, Mary's mother came over and sat beside me. She looked at me with so much love and said "Mary Ellen, I want to thank you so much for visiting Mary in the hospital. Your visit meant so much to her. She changed radically after you left. Mary was filled to overflowing with such a peace and joy that stayed with her till she died. I cannot thank you enough!" My eyes filled with tears because I remembered that I had asked Jesus to stay with her and now I knew that he had. His divine love so filled Mary that she could die in his loving and peaceful presence. The kingdom of God really is now!

We may not have words or fancy gifts to give, but when we have Jesus living in us we have more than we could ever ask for.

If you are now wondering how you can carry Jesus' love to anyone and pass it on, look to Matthew 3:11. It says

> "I am baptizing you with water, for repentance, but the one who is coming after me is mightier than I.
> I am not worthy to carry his sandals. He will baptize you with the holy Spirit and fire."

This is where the three movements of grace – Water, Holy Spirit and Fire appear in our baptism. It is here that we are empowered by God's divine love, to love beyond what we are normally capable of. When we allow the Spirit of God to move in us, he becomes the power and ability to love. We just need to learn how to activate this grace.

Let's now take a closer look at the baptism with water for repentance to see what that has to do with love.

CHAPTER SEVEN

Baptism of Water for Repentance

Before John the Baptist would baptize anyone he exhorted the people to repent and reform. He wanted them to be honest with God about their own sinfulness and selfishness – to take a good hard look at where they had offended God in their life. His whole mission in life was to bring people to repentance and to have an assurance that the people he baptized would reform and change their way of living. We can repent and say we are sorry for our offenses against God, or man, or even ourselves, but it means nothing if we refuse to stop what we are doing and change our behavior – and we can do this only with the help of God. When we repent and reform we let go of the desires in us that are resisting God's love.

The baptism with water for repentance is crucial for walking further with God. It is important to periodically evaluate how we have hurt God, hurt others, hurt ourselves and to forgive those who have injured us – to be brutally honest with ourselves because only the truth will set us free.

In the Sacrament of Baptism, we as Catholics are usually

baptized as infants – washed clean of original sin – the sin of Adam and Eve when they chose their human will instead of the will of God and tried to make themselves equal to God. This arrogance and rebellion is still happening with the children of Adam and Eve today, which is all of us.

Reconciliation and Forgiveness

It isn't until we can discern right from wrong, usually from 6 to 8 years of age, that we become aware of our responsibility to ask God for forgiveness for sin in our lives. We are then encouraged to receive the Sacrament of Reconciliation, and admit to our part of this separation from God. Unfortunately, many of us have taken this grace for granted. We go on sinning without taking responsibility for our actions to God, to ourselves and to others: thus, as we grow older we have accumulated many offenses without repenting and reforming our lives. This is when we need to renew those promises made for us at Baptism.

Many people wonder why we have holy water founts as we enter the doors of Catholic Churches. The water is a reminder of our baptismal vows - as we make the sign of the cross with blessed water we are supposed to remember that we were baptized (washed in water) for the forgiveness of our sins. The water also represents our immersion into the death of Jesus Christ and the coming out of the water as a symbol of Jesus' Resurrection in us. Jesus is the one who stood before the Father and out of his sublime love for us, willingly took upon himself at Calvary the justified wrath of God. The punishment for our rebellion and sinfulness Jesus took for us as he was left alone and abandoned the night before he died. As the nails were driven into his hands and feet our sins were being crucified with him on Calvary, and when he died he took our sins to death with him. When he arose on Easter morning, we too were given new life in

Christ. Jesus did it all out of his extreme love for us. Nobody will ever love us as Jesus loves us. It is his tremendous gift of love for us and we need to appropriate it into our lives by acknowledging our sinfulness and ask him for forgiveness for our part in his suffering. It was not the Roman soldiers or the Jewish leaders who put Jesus on the Cross. It was our willfulness and rebellion that caused Jesus all that pain. I will be forever grateful for the life and death of Jesus, the one who loves mankind beyond our wildest imagination.

During the Lenten season the entire worldwide church is called to spend the 40 days before Easter to evaluate their relationship with God and others. The second precept of the Catholic Church is that we must confess our sins at least once a year, and this is an opportune time. After Lent and during the Easter season, we recommit ourselves to God by renewing our baptismal vows aloud in front of the entire congregation and proclaiming the Nicene Creed as our witness to our faith in the Trinity. The priest then takes blessed water and walks around the church sprinkling the congregation as a reminder of our taking responsibility for our personal sins against God, and of our commitment to our baptismal vows. At the beginning of every Mass we again reflect on possible offenses and confess them together in a short prayer.

As soon as we recognize the fact that we have offended God we need to go to him in prayer and ask him for his forgiveness. If we have hurt another person we should go to them and ask for forgiveness and try to correct the situation. However, sometimes I find that the most difficult one to forgive is myself. Sometimes we can be more punishing to ourselves than to others. It is important however, to forgive ourselves. Without meaningful repentance and a willingness to change, we are effectively choosing to separate ourselves from God and his divine mercy. We are choosing an eternity of alienation from God. By Jesus' sacrifice on Calvary he has atoned for all of our sins if we will allow him to be our Lord and Savior. It is our choice.

Jesus Paid the Price

I once met a "Sky Cap" (a man who helps you with your luggage at the airport) and I noticed a sticker on his cart that read something like, "Jesus Christ Died for You and Me." He saw me reading his sign so I looked at him and said, "He died for me too." Within a few seconds he shared his testimony of being an alcoholic and how God saved him. For years he tried to stop this serious addiction, going in and out of alcohol treatment centers until finally one day while in one of these facilities he became so frustrated because he was getting nowhere, he dropped to his knees, put his hands to his face and sobbed – "God do you hear me??? If you do, please come into my life and take over – I need You!!!" He explained that he experienced such an outpouring of love from God, and an understanding of what Jesus did for him on Calvary. It was then that he became aware of the sin in his life, repented and turned his life in the opposite direction with the help of God.

It was not his will power, emotions, or his intellect that changed him, it was calling out to God from the depth of his spirit and saying, "I need you! Please come into my life and take over!"

I believe the first commandment is the most important because it says, "I am the Lord your God, you shall not have strange gods before me!" When we repent we put God first. All of us have many gods in our lives that are escape hatches, such as unhealthy attachments to people, places, and things; addictions to drugs, alcohol, pornography (and this includes reading sexually explicit novels,) or sexual addictions; power, prestige, and privilege; to name a few. It is the job of the Holy Spirit to reveal to us what they are.

There's So Much More

When we know, we are given the option to hold onto them, or surrender them to God and let him remove them.

This humble man chose to surrender his life and addiction to God and rely on Him to be the God of his life. As he progressed in his walk with God, he began to understand the importance of the blood atonement of Jesus on Calvary and the immense price Jesus paid to gain freedom from sin for us. Jesus gives it to us on a silver platter even though we don't deserve it.

When I think about what Jesus did for me on Calvary and the enormous love he had for me, I picture myself as a slave to sin, standing on the slave traders block up for sale. I would encourage you to stand with me and see what Jesus did for you too.

I was chained to a pole all dirty with torn and filthy clothing (slaves don't take showers every day and don't have fancy clothes). The stench all around me was horrific. As I stood on the block the devil was trying to sell me to the highest bidder.

Then there appeared in the crowd a gentle, compassionate, rich man, named Jesus. He owned the universe and everything in it. He took one look at me and saw the brand mark of Adam and Eve burned into my flesh. He knew that I had been sold into slavery by my first parents, Adam and Eve, and had lived a life of low estate. His eyes began to fill with tears as he saw my deplorable condition. I could see how much he wanted to set me free. Then he spoke up. "How much for Mary Ellen and the rest of these slaves?" The slave trader knew Jesus was interested. "This one will be costly. You'll have to fight me to the death for her." Here was Jesus, the owner of everything good and beautiful. "What did Jesus see in me?" I wondered. "Why would anyone fight to their death for a slave to sin?" I asked myself.

Then the crowds began to move back as Jesus and the slave trader began to fight. The struggle took 3 hours and every drop of blood from Jesus that sprayed over me began to work as a cleanser. As I looked at myself I could see my body, my soul and my spirit being washed and cleansed right before my eyes. His blood was removing the brand mark, and I was clean. His saving and sanctifying blood had such a powerful effect on me.

At first it looked as if Jesus was going to make it but alas he was dead. People walked away from the scene of the crime. His mother and some of his friends picked him up and prepared him for burial. The enemy thought he had won and went away with his friends bragging that he was the winner. I was taken to the detention cell for 2 days with the other slaves. Then all of a sudden Jesus appeared to the slave trader and showed him his hands and feet. "Why do you look so surprised?" Jesus said. "Ghosts don't have flesh and bones as you can see I have. I win! You lose! Now hand them over, they belong to me."

Jesus tied the slave trader and all his friends and marched through town, the victor, dragging them all behind him. I was given my freedom. I'll be forever grateful for the sacrifice of Jesus and the power in his blood to transform me into the woman Jesus knew I could become.

Once Jesus brings us into his kingdom, it is important to remember that we need to stay clean. It is our understanding of the power of the blood and appropriating its power that will keep us walking as free children of God. His blood saves us and sanctifies us. That is why we need to continually evaluate our progress.

As a child growing up I was encouraged to say the Act of Contrition as part of my night prayers. It went something like this: "Oh my God I am sorry for having offended you. I detest all my sins because I dread the loss of heaven and the pains of hell. But most of all because I have sinned against you my God who are all good and deserving of all my love. I detest all my sins and determine with your help, to confess my sins, to do penance and to amend my life. Amen."

Are We Committed to God?

There is another emphasis in water baptism besides confessing sins and turning away from them. It is very important to understand our need for God to be in charge of our life. In Matthew 21:31,32 Jesus was speaking to the chief priests and elders of the people when he said,

> "Amen, I say to you, tax collectors and prostitutes are entering the kingdom of God before you. When John came to you in the way of righteousness, you did not believe him; but tax collectors and prostitutes did. Yet even when you saw that, you did not later change your minds and believe him."

It was because of the faith and humility of the tax collectors and prostitutes that God forgave them. Faith and humility are very important. When we recite the Apostles Creed or the Nicene Creed, we profess our faith in the Trinity. However, at a retreat I recently attended, the presenting priest talked about the word "Creed" and what it meant. We all said it was a statement of our belief. He challenged us and said that the Devil also believed that Jesus was God. What made us different as Christians? He said the word Creed in Greek meant a "commitment to." The tax collectors and prostitutes had appreciation and love for God and committed their lives to Jesus. That's the big difference. Some of us believe that Jesus is Lord, but are we really committed to Jesus and do we allow Jesus to be Lord of our lives in every aspect of it?

One pitch-dark night while sitting on my back patio, I looked up at the stars and planets and wondered how a mere human being like myself could fathom the mind of God – the God who created this immense universe. What was it like to be the God who created such a complicated, intricate and perfectly balanced system of stars and planets? How could I get to know or understand the One who set everything in motion? I felt my mind was way too small to comprehend the mystery of God and his awesome presence in this universe that keeps all things in proper order. As I looked at the magnificent display of grandeur beyond our world I called out to God, "How can I know you? You are so brilliant and beyond anything my mind could ever comprehend." No answer came, so I just continued to experience the beauty around me and to thank God for who he was, and that he created me and placed me along with all living things in such a magnificent setting.

The next day, a thought passed through my mind, "That's why he sent Jesus!" I struggled with this thought because I kept saying to myself, "Great, that was 2,000 years ago! It's too late for me – I never had a chance to meet and talk to Jesus, to ask him about anything." Then I remembered, the words of Jesus were written down in the Bible for the generations that came after his ministry on earth. Perhaps his words would give me a glimpse and help me to understand this awesome mystery.

In John 14:6-11 Jesus said,

> "'I am the way and the truth and the life. No one comes to the Father except through me. If you know me, then you will also know my Father. From now on you do know him and have seen him.' Philip said to him, 'Master, show us the Father, and that will be enough for us.' Jesus said to him, 'Have I been with you for so long a time and you still do not know me, Philip? Whoever has seen me has seen the Father. How can you say, 'Show us the Father'? Do you not believe that I am in the Father and the Father is in me? The words that I speak to

you I do not speak on my own. The Father who dwells in me is doing his works. Believe me that I am in the Father and the Father is in me, or else, believe because of the works themselves.'"

I know this is only a glimpse, but I feel that through reading the Word of God, and developing intimacy with Jesus, through prayer, and the power of the Holy Spirit, I am getting closer to understanding the love of the Father. He loves each one of us, because he is the source of all love and power in the universe. In John 8:31,

"Jesus then said to those Jews who believed in him, 'If you remain in my word, you will truly be my disciples, and you will know the truth, and the truth will set you free.'"

We can see from this scripture that it is extremely important to come to the realization that Jesus really is lord of the universe and that we accept him as our Lord and Savior. Reading about him in scripture helps us to know him better, but a time has to come when we make a decision to say to ourselves "Yes I believe," or "Lord help my unbelief." Many people who make a Cursillo, or attend an Acts Retreat, Emmaus Weekend or Christ Renews His Parish Retreat come to a deeper understanding of what Jesus did for them on the Cross and the grace of their Baptism releases in them.

Let Jesus Be Lord

We need to acknowledge Jesus, commit our lives to him and appreciate the fact that he first loved us to the extent that he died for us. He took upon himself all our individual shame, blame, guilt and punishment that would be directed toward us because of our sinfulness. He then wants to pour out his Holy Spirit on us. Have you done this? Have you cried out to God and said to him, "I want to know you!?" "Please, if you are out there and you hear me, come into my life and help me to know you." I want to encourage you to stop right now, and if you have not invited Jesus to take over and be your lord, do it right now. You may also want to re-commit your life to Jesus. It is very simple. Just say something like, "Dear Jesus, I've heard a lot about you, but I really don't know you personally. I am sorry for all the hurtful things I've done to you and to others (name the people and what you have done) and I ask for forgiveness from you, and someday I'll ask forgiveness from those I have offended, if there is an open door. During my life I have been hurt by others (ask God who they are and then name them) and I choose to forgive them. I ask you to forgive them, and ask you to forgive me for holding onto the grudge for so long. Please put your forgiveness into my heart toward them. Your Word says that what is bound on earth is bound in heaven and what is loosed on earth is loosed in heaven. I want to release all who have hurt me, and I want to be forgiven for all whom I have wounded. I am sorry dear Lord. I want to start all over again and become a new creation in Christ Jesus. I welcome you Lord Jesus into my life, and I ask you to fill me with your Holy Spirit."

In Acts 8:14-17, St. Luke says,

> "Now when the apostles in Jerusalem heard that Samaria had accepted the word of God, they sent them Peter and John, who went down and prayed for them, that they might receive the holy Spirit, for it had not yet fallen upon any of them; they had only been baptized in the name of the Lord Jesus. Then they laid hands on them and they received the holy Spirit."

Here we can see the need for repentance and conversion to Jesus. What happened after that? The apostles came and then, "laid hands on them and they received the holy Spirit." This is why I believe we need to ask for the in-filling of the Holy Spirit after we make the decision to commit to and follow Jesus.

CHAPTER EIGHT

The Baptism of the Holy Spirit

Why is it necessary to ask for the Baptism of the Holy Spirit? I can hear some of you saying, "I did that at my Confirmation," and some of you who have been ordained are probably saying, "I'm ordained. I don't need that. I had hands laid on me at ordination." No doubt some of you are already releasing the power of the Holy Spirit in your life. God knows our hearts, honors our desires, and moves as we give him permission. What I question is where is the evidence that we are walking in the Spirit? When we lay hands on the sick, do they recover? Do you sometimes feel stuck and wonder if God will ever use you? The Baptism of the Holy Spirit is for everyone. When the Spirit descended on Jesus at the Jordan river after he was baptized by John the Baptist in water, Mark 1:10 tells us,

> "On coming up out of the water he (John) saw the heavens being torn open and the Spirit, like a dove, descending upon him (Jesus)."

This was the beginning of the power that moved Jesus in his ministry. We know that he then left there and spent 40 days in the desert, after which he began his mission in the power of the Holy Spirit. For the following 3 years he used this power to bring about the kingdom of God. When Jesus returned to Galilee after his baptism, he went to the synagogue and was handed a scroll, which he read.

> "The Spirit of the LORD is upon me,
> because he has anointed me
> to bring glad tidings to the poor.
> He has sent me to proclaim liberty to
> captives
> and recovery of sight to the blind,
> to let the oppressed go free,
> and to proclaim a year acceptable to the
> LORD."
> (Luke 4:18-19)

This was Jesus' mission after he was baptized. He commissioned us to complete the work he began and he gave us the tools to do the work in the form of the Holy Spirit given to us at Pentecost.

Upon meeting Jesus, John told his followers that although he (John) baptized with water for repentance, Jesus would baptize with the Holy Spirit and fire. I have come to realize that this "baptism" is not a separate baptism, but rather a release of the power of the Spirit that we received in our sacramental reception of Baptism and Confirmation. The Apostles experienced this release at Pentecost and each of us can experience our own Pentecost when we invite the Holy Spirit to come into our lives, and for some of us, to come more deeply into our lives.

The Gifts of the Spirit

When we ask the Holy Spirit to come alive in us, he empowers us with special ministerial gifts to build up the Body of Christ and to accomplish the work set before us. Some of these gifts are mentioned in 1 Corinthians 12:8-11.

> "To one is given through the Spirit the expression of wisdom; to another the expression of knowledge according to the same Spirit;"
> (1Cor. 12:8)

These word gifts of wisdom, knowledge, understanding and counsel are insights for a specific instance. It doesn't mean we have wisdom, it means that when we need to know something, the Holy Spirit will put the word into our mind for the good of someone else. Paul continues in 1 Corinthians 12:9,

> "to another faith by the same Spirit; to another gifts of healing by the one Spirit;"

This faith is given at times when we need an extra measure of faith when facing a particular situation.

> "to another mighty deeds; (such as miracles) to another prophecy; to another discernment of spirits; to another varieties of tongues; to another interpretation of tongues. But one and the same Spirit produces all of these, distributing them individually to each person as he wishes."
> (1 Cor.12:10,11)

The gifts of tongues and interpretation will be further explained in the next chapter. These gifts are not limited to those mentioned by Paul in 1 Corinthians 12 because it is the Holy Spirit who is the gift giver and he knows how he wants to minister through us. We might use one gift one day, and another gift on a different occasion. We need to be open all the time for his will to be completed in us by using all the gifts that the Spirit may give us.

Some other gifts of ministry mentioned in Ephesians 4:11-12, are more comparable to positions.

> "And he gave some as apostles, others as prophets, others as evangelists, others as pastors and teachers, to equip the holy ones for the work of ministry, for building up the body of Christ."

I want to caution against locking into just one of the gifts and thinking you only need this one gift to fulfill God's plan for you. The Holy Spirit is very fluid, and wants us to be open to any of the gifts and be ready to use any one of them whenever he wants.

When we receive the Baptism of the Holy Spirit we receive the same power that Jesus had to heal the brokenhearted, give sight to the blind, and set the captives free. In John 14:12 Jesus says,

> "Amen, amen, I say to you, whoever believes in me will do the works I do, and will do greater ones than these, because I am going to the Father."

No matter what your position is in the church or your social strata, God wants, and is able, to use you by giving you more of the Holy Spirit. When you begin to listen to and obey the Holy Spirit he knows he can trust you with more of his gifts. The gifts are nothing more than the utilization of the power of the Holy Spirit in your life. His movement is reflected in the ways we choose to allow him freedom in us. The Holy Spirit is extremely powerful and as we submit our minds and hearts to him, he will be able to accomplish his will and purpose for our lives and the people he places in our lives. He is only limited by our lack of surrender and inability to be humble.

Are We Using the Power of the Spirit?

Unfortunately, most people still have either no information about what the Holy Spirit wants to do in them, or they have bad information. Sometimes we want the Spirit but only in the way that we have experienced him before. We limit his ability to work with power in us. When I was younger I was comfortable with the Spirit when he helped me with my tests or gave me words to speak at work, but that was the limit of my openness. We need to know that he gives us his ministerial gifts in order to accomplish and finish the work Jesus began. Many Catholics want to take care of their obligation to go to Mass on Sunday and that's it. I have personally heard statements like, "Don't make me sing, don't make me shake hands with the person next to me, don't ask me to do anything for God – I'm too busy." These people really believe that all God expects is for them to be faithful by going to Mass on Sundays, and beyond that, they have no responsibility for bringing change to a world suffering from physical, mental or spiritual starvation.

Our church mentions the importance of using these gifts – sometimes called charisms - in sections 799 and 800 of the <u>Catechism of the Catholic Church</u> (Doubleday, New York, NY, copyright 1994). It says,

> "799 Whether extraordinary or simple and humble, charisms are graces of the Holy Spirit which directly or indirectly benefit the Church, ordered as they are to her building up, to the good of

men, and to the needs of the world.

800 Charisms are to be accepted with gratitude by the person who receives them and by all members of the Church as well. They are a wonderfully rich grace for the apostolic vitality and for the holiness of the entire Body of Christ, provided they really are genuine gifts of the Holy Spirit and are used in full conformity with authentic promptings of this same Spirit, that is, in keeping with charity, the true measure of all charisms."

In order to receive the real blessings of the Baptism of the Holy Spirit we must have child-like faith – in other words – real humility. You don't need a college degree to use the charisms of the Holy Spirit. I have heard people say they are not holy enough and that this grace is only for a selected few who lead exemplary lives. This saddens me because if people really believe this, they will never want or expect to receive all that God has for them. There is so much more for all of us, but it takes humility and trust in God. The Holy Spirit needs us to want and ask for his graces because he will not force himself upon us. Jesus said in Matthew 18:4,5,

> "Whoever humbles himself like this child is the greatest in the kingdom of heaven. And whoever receives one child such as this in my name receives me."

So don't expect only the most respected member of church to be using the gifts. They are given to ordinary people who are willing to be used. Look for the humble people – the people who are surrendered to God to be used in any way he wants to use them.

Surrender to God

We have to surrender our mind and heart to God. What blocks the movement of the Holy Spirit in many people is that they want to use their mind to reach God, when in reality, God is spirit and wants to reign in our spirit. It is so important to surrender. We surrender to what we think and surrender to what we feel. Most people operate in their soul – which is their intellect, will power and emotions – not in their spirit. We are made of body, soul and spirit and, it is in our spirit, that the Spirit of God resides. It is in the inner most core of our being, the spirit, not the body, not the soul, but in the spirit, that the Spirit of God reigns and wants to communicate in, with and through us.

It is curious to me that in Acts 1:3-5, St. Luke wrote that it was 40 days after the Resurrection – that,

> "He presented himself alive to them by many proofs after he had suffered, appearing to them during forty days and speaking about the kingdom of God. While meeting with them, he enjoined them not to depart from Jerusalem, but to wait for 'the promise of the Father about which you have heard me speak; for John baptized with water, but in a few days you will be baptized with the holy Spirit.'"

Perhaps waiting those 40 days was their desert experience, just as Jesus experienced – that place of uncertainty, confusion, isolation and surrender. Notice that Jesus said that "John baptized with water" and in a few days you will be "baptized with the holy Spirit."

In Acts 1:8, Jesus also said,

> "But you will receive POWER when the holy Spirit

comes upon you, and you will be my witnesses in Jerusalem, throughout Judea and Samaria, and to the ends of the earth" (emphasis added).

Modern Day Apostles

Jesus told the apostles and disciples to wait in Jerusalem until they received the promise of the Father - the power of the Holy Spirit. Without the power of the Holy Spirit they would not be able to accomplish the mission he had for them. Pope Paul VI said that the Church exists to evangelize, but do we realize that we desperately need this grace of the release of the Holy Spirit in us to bring the Good News? How can we be lay apostles without the power that only the Holy Spirit can give in this Baptism of the Holy Spirit? In his document <u>On Evangelization in the Modern World,</u> Pope Paul VI says, in section 75,

> "It is in the 'consolation of the Holy Spirit' that the Church increases. The Holy Spirit is the soul of the Church. It is He who explains to the faithful the deep meaning of the teaching of Jesus and of His mystery. It is the Holy Spirit who, today just as at the beginning of the Church, acts in every evangelizer who allows himself to be possessed and led by Him. The Holy Spirit places on his lips the words which he could not find by himself, and at the same time the Holy Spirit predisposes the soul of the hearer to be open and receptive to the Good News and to the kingdom being proclaimed.
>
> Techniques of evangelization are good, but even the most advanced ones could not replace the gentle action of the Spirit. The most perfect preparation of the evangelizer has no effect without the

Holy Spirit. Without the Holy Spirit the most convincing dialectic has no power over the heart of man. Without Him the most highly developed schemas resting on a sociological or psychological basis are quickly seen to be quite valueless."

Unexpected People and Places

The Spirit moves where and when he wants to the most unexpected places and to the most unexpected people. In the story of Cornelius, the Roman centurion, in Acts 10:2 it says that he was

> "devout and God-fearing along with his whole household, who used to give alms generously to the Jewish people and pray to God constantly."

While at prayer one day he had a vision of an angel who told him to send for Peter who was staying with Simon, a tanner, who lived by the sea. So he sent some servants to bring Peter to him. Meanwhile Peter was at prayer on his roof terrace and fell into a trance. In Acts 10:11-15 it says,

> "He saw heaven opened and something resembling a large sheet coming down, lowered to the ground by its four corners. In it were all the earth's four-legged animals and reptiles and the birds of the sky. A voice said to him, 'Get up, Peter. Slaughter and eat.' But Peter said, 'Certainly not, sir. For never have I eaten anything profane and unclean.' The voice spoke to him again, a second time, 'What God has made clean, you are not to call profane.'"

While he was pondering the meaning of this, the servants arrived to ask him to go to Cornelius. On the following day

Peter and some of the brothers went with them to Caesarea. Cornelius was waiting for them and had called together his relatives and close friends. In Acts 10: 28, 29 Peter said to them,

> "You know that it is unlawful for a Jewish man to associate with, or visit, a Gentile, but God has shown me that I should not call any person profane or unclean. And that is why I came without objection when sent for. May I ask, then, why you summoned me?"

Then Cornelius explained the vision he had during his prayer time when he was told to send for Peter. Cornelius said in Acts 10:33,

> "So I sent for you immediately, and you were kind enough to come. Now therefore we are all here in the presence of God to listen to all that you have been commanded by the Lord."

Further on in Acts 10:44-49 it says,

> "While Peter was still speaking these things, the holy Spirit fell upon all who were listening to the word. The circumcised believers who had accompanied Peter were astounded that the gift of the holy Spirit should have been poured out on the Gentiles also, for they could hear them speaking in tongues and glorifying God. Then Peter responded, 'Can anyone withhold the water for baptizing these people, who have received the holy Spirit even as we have?' He ordered them to be baptized in the name of Jesus Christ. Then they invited him to stay for a few days."

When Peter went to Jerusalem the Jewish believers confronted him about entering the house of uncircumcised people and eating with them. Peter explained all that had happened to him and continued in Acts 11:15-18.

> "As I began to speak, the holy Spirit fell upon them as it had upon us at the beginning, and I remembered the word of the Lord, how he had said, 'John baptized with water but you will be baptized with the holy Spirit.' If then God gave them the same gift he gave to us when we came to believe in the Lord Jesus Christ, who was I to be able to hinder God?' When they heard this, they stopped objecting and glorified God, saying, 'God has then granted life-giving repentance to the Gentiles too.' "

Baptism of Water, Holy Spirit and Fire

Previously I mentioned that I believe there are three dimensions of baptism – water, Holy Spirit and fire and it doesn't matter in what order they are received or appropriated. Here you can see that the Spirit moved in the baptism of the Holy Spirit first (the sign was that they were speaking in tongues and glorifying God). Then what did Peter do next?

> "He ordered them to be baptized in the name of Jesus Christ."
> (Acts 10:48)

This was the baptism of water. Then as they stay faithful to Jesus and use their gifts for the honor of God they grow in holiness.

The important issue here is not when or how you release in the Holy Spirit - belief first with water baptism and then release of the gifts of the Holy Spirit. The underlying fact was that they were humble and had faith that God would move on them. They loved and honored God (even though they were not Jewish) and because of their humility and faith, God rewarded them with revealing the fullness of the Holy Spirit. The baptism of the Holy Spirit is using all the gifts the Spirit wants to give us, to build up the body of Christ. The gifts are for all of us. In 1 Corinthians 12:4-7 St. Paul says,

> "There are different kinds of spiritual gifts but the same Spirit; there are different forms of service but the same Lord; there are different workings but the same God who produces all of them in everyone. To each individual the manifestation of the Spirit is given for some benefit."

The Holy Spirit is the Gift and Gift-Giver

The Holy Spirit helps us appropriate the gifts when he knows there is a need and knows that we are open to cooperate with him. When I look at the gifts my concern is that we may become focused on the gifts rather than the "Giver" of the gifts. The Holy Spirit knows what gifts we need and when to manifest himself through these gifts. Too often we may feel that we don't have a specific gift. If we know they are available to us and if the Holy Spirit wants to, he can manifest a specific gift when it is needed through us if we are willing to have confidence that he can do it and feel it is his will.

The main idea I want to impart is that we need to be attuned to the Holy Spirit and have an ongoing relationship with him through our prayer life, so that we may be available to him when he wants to move.

Ask for More of the Holy Spirit

St. Paul wants and expects us to have the ministerial gifts of the Holy Spirit especially the gifts that help us to be able to explain the mission of Jesus and his power, such as prophecy, a word of wisdom, knowledge, understanding and counsel. I hear people say, "I don't need the gifts of the Holy Spirit – I have love and that's more important." Then they quote 1 Corinthians 13. This shows me that they have never read 1 Corinthians 12, because Paul assumes the people already have the ministerial gifts of the Holy Spirit. In 1 Corinthians 14:1 Paul urges us,

> "to strive eagerly for the spiritual gifts, above all that you may prophesy."

Jesus wants us to desire and use all the gifts of the Holy Spirit. That's why he told his apostles and disciples to wait in Jerusalem until the Holy Spirit comes with his gifts. There would not be a church without the gifts. It is not possible to evangelize without the power that comes from the ministerial gifts of the Holy Spirit. The Spirit wants us to use all his gifts to bring about the kingdom.

It is possible to be using some of the gifts of the Holy Spirit and not be fully released in the fullness of the Spirit just as I experienced after attending a few prayer meetings. Remember I said that I was praying in tongues months before I asked for the release of the Holy Spirit? I believe that was because I desired more intimacy with God in prayer and so that was one of the gifts that released easily in me – I was open to it. When I went to Notre Dame and when people prayed for me and laid their hands on me for the full release of the gifts of the Holy Spirit, I was open to so much more. I was willing to surrender all for God. The Holy Spirit was far more generous than I ever dreamed of.

I never imagined what he had in store for me.

You may see in your own life gifts that have been releasing through the years. You may have the gift of exhortation, teaching, administration or even healing, but not be fully released in the power of the Holy Spirit. There is always so much more. We need to be humble and ask the Holy Spirit to pour out more of himself on us. He is the giver of all the ministerial gifts and all the sanctifying gifts. He desperately wants us to ask for them, but sometimes we are afraid of what it will mean to our comfortable little world if we get them. I would encourage you to look into the face of God (love) and know that he has a much better plan for us than we could ever hope for or imagine. His perfect love is aching for us to receive more of him. Please, don't be afraid. The Holy Spirit is so gentle and kind and he knows us better than we know ourselves. Make a promise to yourself before you ask for more, that you will use all the gifts he gives you to the best of your ability, for his honor and glory.

Each morning during my prayer time, I recommit myself to Jesus as my Lord and Savior. I then ask for a fresh in-filling of the Holy Spirit, and for revival (sanctification) in myself and in the church. In other words, I pray for a fresh anointing of Matthew 3:11 – Jesus' Lordship over my life (water baptism); further release of the Holy Spirit (Holy Spirit baptism) and sanctifying revival (fire baptism).

Prayer Meetings are a Venue for Using Your Gifts

The gifts of the Holy Spirit mentioned in the Catholic Catechism were called Charisms. I spoke before of going to a Charismatic prayer meeting where I learned to open up to the presence of God more fully and began to release in the Holy Spirit and to use his gifts. When I go to a prayer meeting where the people are open to the movement of the Holy Spirit through his charisms I always come home refreshed and energized. A good prayer meeting consists of singing praise for about 30 minutes in your own language and in tongues. There should be a prophetic exhortation in tongues with an interpretation. People should be willing to share how the Lord used them during the week or an important scripture that had a specific effect on them. All members should be encouraged to share a word, a thought, or a spiritual image. When this pattern is followed, a theme will evolve and you can actually come to an understanding of what the Spirit is saying to your community. It also helps if someone writes down the various messages that come from the members and reads them back to the group at the end of the meeting. It cements the idea the Holy Spirit is trying to say.

All gifts, except the gift of tongues, are given for ministry to others. (Only when tongues are interpreted is it for the community.) When we pray in tongues we are allowing the Holy Spirit to pray his mind rather than ours. When I pray only with my mind, I feel I am limiting the Holy Spirit. Tongues is a wonderful prayer language and St. Paul reminds us in 1 Corinthians 14:18, that,

> "I give thanks to God that I speak in tongues more than any of you."

So if St. Paul prays in tongues, more than any of you, he is saying it is very important, and expects the believers to be praying in tongues as often as they can.

He also wants the other ministerial gifts to be used such as prophecy, and words of wisdom, knowledge and understanding, so the unbelievers in the crowd may come to know the truth about Jesus as Lord and God. Paul mentions in 1 Corinthians 12:31 after naming the gifts of the Spirit,

> "Strive eagerly for the greatest spiritual gifts.
> But I shall show you a still more excellent

way."

Then he goes on in chapter 13 to encourage them to remember that everything revolves around love. This passage was written to believers who were released in the power of the Holy Spirit and manifesting the gifts of the Holy Spirit. He was talking to people who had the baptism with water and the release of the Holy Spirit. He assumed the believers were manifesting the ministerial gifts of the Holy Spirit.

The Spirit of Divine Love

That's why I believe the third dimension, the baptism of fire is so important, for it releases the power of the Holy Spirit to sanctify us - to make us into vessels of his Divine love. All my life I tried to love in my own power, but kept falling short. Now I know that it must be only in the power of the Holy Spirit or I get really frustrated. Now I let the Holy Spirit move his Divine love through me and it is so much easier. The greatest evidence of the Holy Spirit is his love flowing through us. We cannot do this on our own power. It is so important to allow the Holy Spirit free reign in our lives. He is the one with the power!

If we use the ministerial gifts of the Holy Spirit properly and for the glory of God, we should start to manifest the fruits of the Holy Spirit mentioned in Galatians 5:22-23.

> "In contrast, the fruit of the Spirit is love, joy, peace, patience, kindness, generosity, faithfulness, gentleness, self-control."

What's the first fruit of the Spirit? Love. There it is. The love Paul talks about in 1 Corinthians 13 and Galatians 5:22. When we use the gifts of the Holy Spirit properly we should start to manifest the fruits – love, joy, peace, etc. This is not a human love. It is a divine love! Only when you experience and I say that word again, experience, God's love for you will you ever be able to love God, yourself or others in a fuller, more meaningful way. Paul understood that there was a difference because he could discern who was filled with this kind of love and who was not. You may have a gift or several gifts that you use. But unless you have experienced repentance, having forgiven those who hurt you, and are allowing Jesus to be Lord of your life, and continually ask the Holy Spirit to fill you each day, you will have a difficult time loving as Jesus loved.

Is your love a phony love, a natural love, or is it empowered by the Holy Spirit? There is a big difference. The phony love is a conditional love and looks to see if you are getting love back, always checking the motive and is driven by fear. The natural love requires no effort because there is no depth. The divine love of the Holy Spirit flows through you to reach out to those who don't deserve your love, and are transformed by his presence in your life. You become a stream of living water refreshing the people around you, without you even realizing it. It is not you, it is the presence of the Holy Spirit moving through you reaching out to the wounded and lost, the sick and afraid, bringing healing and wholeness – but most of all – a sense that they are loved.

Love Activates the Holy Spirit

Many say that love activates the movement of grace. When you care about someone it seems to carry the movement of the Holy Spirit more easily. One day we received a phone call from the woman who played the music for our prayer group. She said her husband had been to the emergency room at their local hospital in severe pain and when they x-rayed him they found dark shadows on his intestines and were worried about tumors. We were all concerned because a number of years earlier, he had breast cancer, which is very rare in men. Since he was a veteran, he entered the Veteran hospital nearby our home and they also confirmed the diagnosis with another set of x-rays.

Our friend said her husband was to have a biopsy the next morning to determine if the tumors were malignant and asked us if we would pray for him. Since Ray's office was not far from the hospital I called Ray and met him at work and we drove over to the hospital together to visit our friend. At the end of our visit, we asked him if he would like us to pray with him for good results. We all prayed for a few minutes.

The next night, we were at the prayer meeting and we saw our friend with some other people in the prayer group and she was crying. We felt so sad because we figured the results were bad. We walked over to her apprehensively expecting the worst. When she lifted her head and saw us she explained that her tears were tears of joy because they did not find cancer, only scar tissue. There was no evidence of tumors. They dismissed him from the hospital and he never had the problem again. So you can see whatever the Holy Spirit wants to do, he can and will do, if we will just cooperate with him. He just needs our willingness to step out in faith even if it makes us look foolish.

Of all the gifts of the Holy Spirit, I hear more opposition to the gift of tongues, so I would like to try to help you understand it more clearly. Hopefully you will desire this precious gift, ask the Holy Spirit for it, and use it, for the body of Christ and to enhance your unique love relationship with God

CHAPTER NINE

The Gift of Tongues

One of the gifts of the Holy Spirit is a prayer language, the gift of tongues. St. Paul tells us in Romans 8:26, 27 about this gift.

> "In the same way, the Spirit too comes to the aid of our weakness; for we do not know how to pray as we ought, but the Spirit itself intercedes with inexpressible groanings.
> And the one who searches hearts knows what is the intention of the Spirit, because it intercedes for the holy ones according to God's will."

Praying in tongues is a prayer language that allows the Spirit to pray in and through us. The gift of tongues comes from the depths of our beings – with groaning that comes from deep within making sounds that bypass our intellect, will power and emotions. Tongues give us freedom in our spirit – nothing is held back, and sets us free to praise, worship, thank, confess and petition God like no other gift.

It saddens me to see that many people receive this precious gift and toss it aside – never - or rarely ever using it. I would like to encourage you to ask God for this wonderful gift and to use it every day. Most of the time we pray to God, only in our finite mind. We focus on asking God for our wants and needs and our words are limited by our vocabulary. I feel we look at a problem through a keyhole, and God looks at the same problem from inside the room. Our mind is wonderful. We have intelligence, and our emotions are real. However, when I pray in tongues, I am allowing the Holy Spirit to look at the entire picture and intercede for me to my heavenly Father, through Jesus, the way he wants. In other words, I am surrendering how I think it should be done and asking God to do it his way.

We are made up of: body; soul – (which is our intellect, will power and emotions); and spirit. When we are baptized, the Spirit of God comes to us and resides in our spirit. He is either free to manifest his desires, or is held bound by our ignorance or arrogance. When we use our mind (soul) and body to figure things out, we often fall short of God's divine plan for our lives.

In John 4:23-24, Jesus was speaking to the Samaritan woman when he said,

> "But the hour is coming, and is now here, when true worshipers will worship the Father in Spirit and truth; and indeed the Father seeks such people to worship him. God is Spirit, and those who worship him must worship in Spirit and truth."

The Spirit Speaks Through Us

I was at my third prayer meeting and while singing praise to God in English, I began to release in tongues. I knew little about this gift, and when it happened I was very surprised. While driving home in the car I sang in tongues all the way home. I didn't want to stop praising God but I had four young children who would be waking up around 6:30 a.m. It was well after midnight when I drew the covers over myself. I was concerned that if I stopped using this wonderful gift, I might lose it. I asked the Holy Spirit not to leave, and in the morning when I awoke his praise was still on my lips.

That occurred on March 30th. I never had hands laid on me for the release of the Holy Spirit until I went to the conference at Notre Dame University in June. (Meanwhile I had been praying in tongues during April and May). It was at Notre Dame that I asked Jesus to be my Lord and Savior and asked for his Divine Love to fill me. It was at the conference that I surrendered my life to him, and repented of what I had done in my life.

I attended the conference with five other members of my prayer group – my aunt, who was a Dominican nun, a Chinese priest, the lay woman leader of the prayer group and a lay man and woman. On the way home as we drove from Kennedy airport to my house out on Long Island, the Chinese priest asked for prayers. He had been born and raised in China and when the Communists invaded China he had to leave because he was in the seminary, and priests and sisters were being killed. His sister was a nun and they both lived in Taiwan. He was a diocesan priest in Taipei who was studying for his doctorate in Rome and ministered in a church on Long Island during the summers to help support his studies.

We pulled up to the curb in my neighborhood and the leader asked me to pray over Fr. Peter, since I recently had hands laid on me at the conference for the release of the Holy Spirit. I was sitting in the front seat and turned around – kneeling, facing the back of the car with my hand reaching over Fr. Peter's head. I didn't know what was on his heart so I just prayed in tongues.

The next week I saw Fr. Peter at the prayer meeting and he came over to me and told me what had occurred the night

I prayed over him. He said, "You won't believe what happened. When I arrived home I sat down and wrote the sounds that you made when you prayed over me. Mary Ellen, you were praying in Mandarin Chinese and it was the answer to my prayers." He normally spoke a different dialect, but knew Mandarin. He also said that the presence of God was so strong in his room that night, that he felt Jesus was sitting on his bed.

At each prayer meeting while I was in New York, Fr. Peter made a point to sit next to me. Sometimes I felt he was waiting to see if God would use me again to speak to him in Chinese. Unfortunately, it never happened again. We moved to Miami a few months later, but we remain close friends to this day. I feel God was teaching me a good lesson. When I went to the conference I had the attitude that since I had the gift of tongues, I wanted to move onto the higher gifts such as healing, miracles, prophecy, etc. I hadn't honored my gift of tongues and said to myself, "I know what I want to pray for, I have a good mind, I can talk to God very clearly." In reality, I wanted to use my mind instead of my spirit.

Peter on the other hand was very lonesome for his Chinese people. Little did I realize that God wanted me to value this precious gift, and that even though there were not many Chinese people on Long Island, God gave Fr. Peter some one who spoke Chinese to him, even though I didn't know Chinese.

When some people pray for the release of the Holy Spirit and his gifts, they expect to be zapped with a foreign language that they may be familiar with. However, we need to leave that up to God to see if he wants to use your language in that way. My experience with Father Peter is not the norm. I would encourage you to begin by giving God syllables that come from your heart and bypass your mind. He will do the rest.

Freedom to Praise

When we allow the Holy Spirit freedom to pray through us it is much different than using our minds. I find it so much easier to pray in tongues, because I don't have to remember to say certain things. I can pray all day long. Tongues are especially great when you are folding your laundry. When all of our children were home, I could sort and fold clothes, deciding on which child's pile to put each pair of socks, while I prayed in tongues through my spirit. I didn't need my thinking capacity to pray. I used my mind to figure out which piece of clothing belonged to whom. My body folded and placed it in the right pile, but my spirit was busy praising and worshipping God. God wants us to praise him through our spirit.

Jesus, himself, said that our worship must come from our spirit, with the help of the Holy Spirit. I hope you will take this to heart, and ask God to give you this great gift. He can pray for, in, and through us, setting us free in his truth. We need to quiet down and let the Holy Spirit move in us as he so much wants to.

I knew of a woman who read the psalms aloud every day. As she prayed the psalms, she began to make some strange sounds while reading. This disturbed her greatly, because she felt that perhaps she was losing her mind. This phenomena happened only when she read the psalms. Sometime later she attended a charismatic prayer meeting and heard several people making similar sounds and found that they were speaking in tongues. When she went back to reading the psalms she let the Spirit flow, and realized she had received the gift of tongues even before she knew anything about it.

What is holding us back? Have we not really surrendered all to Jesus? Have we not forgiven all who have wounded us? It is so simple – but it takes a great deal of humility! When I heard my husband first speak in tongues I felt embarrassed. We were at a prayer meeting and people, including my husband, were praying over me in proxy for my sister. I was sitting on a chair and as they prayed in tongues over me I heard my husband praying in tongues, along with the others, with sounds that reminded me of a child in a crib saying, "da, da, da, or ba, ba, ba." At the time he was a pilot for Pan American Airlines and I thought he and I were quite sophisticated. I felt embarrassed for him and embarrassed for myself that I had a husband who sounded like an infant. That's what I mean – it takes humility – and an ability to be willing to be a fool for Christ. I thank God he had the humility. His prayer language now, 30 years later, is much more refined and I am so grateful that he uses it everyday.

Jesus sent us the Holy Spirit to pray in and through our spirits to the Father. That's why he told his disciples to wait for the Holy Spirit. If we refuse to worship in spirit and truth, are we saying we don't want to do it God's way? In Hebrews 7:25 it says,

> "Therefore, he (Jesus) is always able to save those who approach God through him, since he lives forever to make intercession for them."

So we know that Jesus is constantly interceding for us before the throne of his father. When we pray in the spirit (tongues), the Holy Spirit is set free to speak to Jesus, so that Jesus can intercede the mind of God to the Father for us - not our mind, but his mind.

Seeking And Using The Gifts

I know this sounds strong, but I am very concerned that since 1967 the Holy Spirit has been poured out on the Catholic Church like no other time in history, and yet so few people have responded with open hearts and minds to the prompting of the Holy Spirit. He wants us to use his gifts. He wants to be released in us. He wants to accomplish so much in us. He wants to empower us to pray and praise his way. The power to love is released in tongues. In 1 John 4:13 we see that the Spirit is God's sign of love to us.

> "This is how we know that we remain in him
> and he in us, that he has given us of his Spirit."

Are we too busy for intimacy? Do we feel it is just not that important? Do we just want to pray our own way? Have we let this wonderful gift die from lack of use? This reminds me of a seed falling on hard ground. If this has happened to you, I would encourage you to humble yourself and ask God to give you a fresh in-filling and release once more the gift of tongues and then promise yourself you'll never stop using it. It is a gift, just like faith, and God wants you to have it and use it. You alone have to appropriate the gift. If you have never received this gift because you never knew about it, please don't be afraid. God really wants to release in you all his gifts and even though this is not one of the higher gifts it is invaluable to your prayer life and intimacy with God.

Jesus commissioned us – all of us – when he said in Mark 16:15-17,

> "Go into the whole world and proclaim the gospel to every creature. Whoever believes and is baptized will be saved; whoever does not believe will be condemned. These signs will accompany those who believe: in my name they will drive out demons, they will speak new languages."

Jesus sent the Holy Spirit to give the Apostles and to all of us the power to proclaim the gospel to every nation. The

Holy Spirit gives us all his gifts, including the gift of tongues, to fulfill Jesus' command "to cast out demons and to lay hands on the sick so that they would recover." The power is in the gifts of the Spirit!

St. Paul said that he prayed in tongues more than any of us (1 Corinthians 14:18). He knew God wanted to be in control of the prayer – not him. If we consider ourselves Christian, are we doing what Jesus commissioned us to do? Are we using our new language to bring God's healing to the wounded and lost, the sick and afraid? Are we using our gift to praise and to adore our heavenly Father?

One night recently, I went to bed early – about 9:30p.m. At about 11:00p.m. I woke up and couldn't go back to sleep, so I got up and began praying. Since I didn't know what I was praying for, I just prayed in tongues. I figured God knew someone, somewhere, needed prayer. I continued praying till around 3:00 a.m. and then returned to bed. The next day I received a telephone call from my son and he told me what had happened the night before. He is a pilot for Delta Airlines and received a call from his wife at 11:00 that night. She was 5 months pregnant and was bleeding. He told her to get to the hospital immediately and he would arrange to take the next flight home. He said she called him back at 3:00 a.m. that morning telling him that the baby had died at 4 months and that she had to go through the delivery knowing her baby was already dead. It was a very sad and frightening time for both of them. However, I believe in my heart that God knew they needed prayer at this really sad time. I knew nothing of this when it was happening, but feel in some small way, the prayers that I said helped them get through.

The gift of tongues is a powerful prayer gift. We need it to do the work God calls us to do and to have true intimacy with him. Without tongues we may miss out on the power of God.

The Power of Pentecost

Jesus told his followers to wait for the Holy Spirit. We know that they returned to Jerusalem and devoted themselves with one accord to prayer, with some women and Mary the mother of Jesus. In Acts 2:1-4 it says,

> "When the time for Pentecost was fulfilled, they were all in one place together. And suddenly there came from the sky a noise like a strong driving wind, and it filled the entire house in which they were. Then there appeared to them tongues as of fire, which parted and came to rest on each one of them. And they were all filled with the holy Spirit and began to speak in different tongues, as the Spirit enabled them to proclaim."

I love to picture Mary, the mother of Jesus, Martha and Mary, Peter, James and John, Mary Magdalene, Thomas and all the other 120 apostles and disciples in a room worshipping and singing the psalms, when all of a sudden the Holy Spirit moved in power upon all of them. What did their faces look like when they began to speak in tongues? Was Jesus' mother, Mary, the first to start singing and praying in tongues or was it John, his best friend, or maybe it was Peter our first pope? I would have loved to have been in the upper room that day. It must have been a glorious sight! Mary has been a role model for me and it's nice to know that I can pray the way Mary prayed.

What happened after that? They were empowered to speak with power and authority helping others to understand that Jesus was the Messiah. When hands were laid on the sick they recovered, people were being set free of physical blindness as well as spiritual blindness, physical deafness as well as spiritual deafness, hearts were being healed, and much more. All came to know that their heavenly Father loved them and had not forsaken them. Soon after Pentecost, Peter was speaking to the crowd and in Acts 2:37-41 it says,

> "Now when they heard this, they were cut to the heart, and they asked Peter and the other apostles, 'What are we to do, my brothers?' Peter [said] to them, 'Repent and be baptized, everyone of you, in the name of Jesus Christ for the forgiveness of your sins; and you will receive the gift of the holy Spirit. For the promise is made to you and to your children and to all those far off, whomever the Lord our God will call.' He testified with many other arguments, and was exhorting them, 'Save yourselves from this corrupt generation.' Those who accepted his message were baptized, and about three thousand persons were added that day."

This was the same Peter who denied Christ during his passion only a few weeks before. Conversions happened because his apostles and disciples were faithful and obedient to Jesus when he said to go into Jerusalem and wait for the Holy Spirit. The first apostles needed the in-filling of the Holy Spirit and this new prayer language. They knew Jesus and had lived with him for years, listening to his teachings, but only now they were filled with power to bring about the kingdom as Jesus did. They could not do this before Pentecost.

So we also in the 21st century need this in-filling of the Holy Spirit that empowers us to pray in tongues and announce the good news, delivering the captives of sin and disease and revealing God's love and mercy.

One day while singing and praying in tongues during my prayer time I began to cough. I figured it was because I was singing and needed a cup of water. As I continued to praise and worship God in tongues the coughing got stronger and stronger. Then I remembered that sometimes God releases us of blockages that hold us back from a deeper walk with him. As I continued to cough I asked God what he was doing. And the word I received was, "Shame, I am delivering you of shame." I questioned him further. "Shame, God, where and when?" Then it came to me, several different times in my life where I experienced shame. I knew from the depths of my being that God was releasing me from shame. Jesus came to set us free. As I continued to praise and worship him in tongues, I kept thanking him for his power that is the same today, as it was 2,000 years ago. I could not stop thanking God that he inhabits the praise of his people and it is in his presence that we receive healing, deliverance, and wholeness.

In Acts 19:1-7 it says,

> "While Apollos was in Corinth, Paul traveled through the interior of the country and came [down] to Ephesus where he found some disciples. He said to them, 'Did you receive the holy Spirit when you became believers?' They answered him, 'We have never even heard that there is a holy Spirit.' He said, 'How were you baptized?' They replied, 'With the baptism of John.' Paul then said, 'John baptized with a baptism of repentance, telling the people to believe in the one who was to come after him, that is, in Jesus.' When they heard this, they were baptized in the name of the Lord Jesus. And when Paul laid [his] hands on them, the holy Spirit came upon them, and they spoke in tongues and prophesied. Altogether there were about twelve men."

Don't Limit The Spirit

As you can see, there are many scriptures that mention that when you receive the Holy Spirit you also receive his gifts. His presence became evident when they "spoke in tongues." Then they had the power to proclaim the message of salvation. If you are in ministry and find it difficult to share your testimony and the message of salvation and would like to see more evidence of the Holy Spirit moving in your life, ask the Spirit to release more in you. When you do this be open to all the gifts of the Holy Spirit. Be prepared to receive your prayer language. You might be at a prayer meeting, in the shower singing to the Lord, or driving to work when the Holy Spirit begins to move in you. Give him permission to do whatever he wants and to give you whatever gifts he wants. He wants to give you all his gifts. When we are willing to receive the gift of tongues, even though we might think it foolish, he will know that he can trust you with the higher gifts.

Continuing in Acts 19:8-12 we read that,

> "He (Paul) entered the synagogue, and for three months debated boldly with persuasive arguments about the kingdom of God. But when some in their obstinacy and disbelief disparaged the Way before the assembly, he withdrew and took his disciples with him and began to hold daily discussions in the lecture hall of Tyrannus. This continued for two years with the result that all the inhabitants of the province of Asia heard the word of the Lord, Jews and Greeks alike. So extraordinary were the mighty deeds God accomplished at the hands of Paul that when face cloths or aprons that touched his skin were applied to the sick, their diseases left them and the evil spirits came out of them."

St. Paul, as you can see, was truly filled with the Holy Spirit and fire! He was not afraid to speak to anyone about Jesus Christ. He was filled with the power that could come only from God. Paul was also refined through the years as he ministered to the people. He learned as he went. God knew he could trust him in all things, because when he gave Paul things to do, he did his best to be faithful and obedient to God. When I say he was refined I want you to think what refined means. Let's now take a look at the baptism of fire – the refining fire.

CHAPTER TEN

Baptism of Fire

All of our journeys are different. We are each unique and individual in our relationship with God. No one comes to God in exactly the same way. Peter was a rough, uneducated, outspoken fisherman who walked and talked with Jesus for several years. Paul was an intellectual with all kinds of "high church" Jewish credentials who hated the first Christians because he thought they were heretical. John was probably a young apostle whom Jesus took under his wing because of the mutual bond of love and respect for each other. Martha and Mary knew him as a close friend, and Mary Magdalene knew Jesus as the image of his heavenly Father, loving and accepting her as she was. The Samaritan woman was not even Jewish, nor was Cornelius who was a Roman centurion.

Jesus revealed his Father's love to all of them; healed their wounds; physically, mentally, and spiritually, and delivered them from the bondage of sin and ignorance in their lives while using them to bring about the kingdom. Each one came from a very different place, yet all of them came into a deep personal relationship with Jesus in their own unique way and in the process grew in holiness. Jesus will do the same for you and me.

When I read the lives of the saints and saw the way God expressed his love to them and how he used them, I remember praying and asking God to make me like them. Some time after I prayed that prayer, I felt God was saying, "Mary Ellen, I don't want or need another Teresa of Avila, or another Catherine of Siena, I want and need a Mary Ellen Farrell Rossman at this time and place in history." I would say the same thing to you. God loves, wants and needs you exactly who and where you are.

I want to encourage you to appreciate your own uniqueness, your own individuality, your own personality and your own personal relationship with Jesus. No two people have the same experience or the same mission. God gives us special talents, and has a plan and purpose for each one of us. He needs you and wants you exactly the way you are. With our cooperation, the Holy Spirit will make us into what he knows we can become. That's what I believe the Baptism of Fire is all about. It's about letting the Holy Spirit sanctify you. He can and wants to make you holy. He will do it if you are willing to cooperate with him and become sensitive to his movement in your life. I believe he is trying to communicate with us all day long. We just need to be listening to him and be observant about what is going on around us. He wants us to notice him.

When I was preparing for Confirmation as a child, my teacher talked about two kinds of grace – actual grace and sanctifying grace. She took the word actual and underlined the first part of the word - act. She said it is an action word, and after Confirmation we should expect the Holy Spirit to help us to act like Christians, to be able to share our faith, and that we should pray to the Holy Spirit for help in our lives. She did not explain to us that the Holy Spirit gives us his ministerial gifts as noted in 1 Cor. 12 to accomplish this task.

Now I realize that this actual grace that my teacher spoke

of is any movement of the Holy Spirit, and is not limited to the charisms. However after years of using the gifts of the Holy Spirit and seeing for myself the importance of these ministerial charisms I have begun to believe that it is important for teachers to tell their students that the Holy Spirit will give them these graces if they ask for them. We need to tell our students that the gifts, such as: a word of wisdom, a word of knowledge, a word of understanding, healing, miracles, discernment, tongues, and interpretation of tongues, are for all of us to help us to act on the movement of the Holy Spirit in our lives. I believe that is what we call the Baptism of the Holy Spirit. It is grace for ministry. Some day you might be speaking to someone and as the Spirit moves through you a word of wisdom, knowledge or understanding may flow out of your mouth without you ever thinking about it, and it will have a healing effect on the one you are speaking to. This is not a sign of holiness. It is a sign that you are willing to be used by the Holy Spirit at a specific time.

My Confirmation teacher did talk about the sanctifying gifts of the Holy Spirit – wisdom, knowledge, understanding, piety, fortitude, counsel and fear of the Lord. These are gifts given for personal holiness – for you and for me to live holy sanctified lives. The prophet Isaiah speaks of these gifts in chapter 11:2,3.

> "The spirit of the LORD shall rest upon him:
> a spirit of wisdom and of understanding,
> A spirit of counsel and of strength,
> a spirit of knowledge and of fear of the LORD,
> and his delight shall be the fear of the LORD."

The Baptism of Fire is the sanctifying grace my teacher was talking about. When you think of fire what do you conjure up in your mind? Fire purifies elements such as gold. The ore has to be heated up to extract the gold – pure gold. I believe God is doing a sanctifying work today. He wants to purify our life and empower us to live holy lives. I believe there is a revival going on now, and that it will be more powerful and more wide spread than any previous movement of grace.

God's presence is described as fire many times in the scriptures. In Acts 2:1-3, it says,

> "When the time for Pentecost was fulfilled, they were all in one place together. And suddenly there came from the sky a noise like a strong driving wind, and it filled the entire house in which they were. Then there appeared to them tongues as of fire, which parted and came to rest on each one of them."

It wasn't until they experienced Pentecost that they were empowered to live the life Jesus called them to. They were given the sanctifying gifts of the Holy Spirit, and were enabled to live a life of holiness – a life focused on Jesus! They began to understand that Jesus was the sacrificial offering, the Lamb that was slain. They understood that Jesus was our atonement for all the sin, guilt and shame in our lives and that he could deliver anyone from what binds them by the power of his shed blood. They lived lives of fervent faith, hope and love. They experienced God's presence, which convicts and delivers us from sin. The tongues of fire marked the presence of God and his ability to create a holy people.

We Need His Power

If you take a good look at your life and watch your response to crisis you will have a good idea where you stand spiritually. Listen to the people around you and see what they say about you. Sometimes there is a grain of truth to their accusations. When we humble ourselves before the Lord and allow the Holy Spirit to change us he will be able to trust us with more of his power.

St. Paul says in 1 Corinthians 2:3-5,

> "I came to you in weakness and fear and much trembling, and my message and my proclamation were not with persuasive [words of] wisdom, but with a demonstration of spirit and power, so that your faith might rest not on human wisdom but on the <u>power of God</u>" (emphasis added).

God wants us sanctified so that he may give us more of his power! Without the power of God, we remain impotent to reveal his loving presence to this world. We can talk endlessly, but unless the power of God is revealed, we'll neither be convinced, nor convince anyone of God's reality and the wonders he has prepared for us.

In 1 Corinthians 2:10-14 Paul continues,

> "For the Spirit scrutinizes everything, even the depths of God. Among human beings, who knows what pertains to a person except the spirit of the person that is within? Similarly, no one knows what pertains to God except the Spirit of God. We have not received the spirit of the world but the Spirit that is from God, so that we may understand the things freely given us by God. And we speak about them not with words taught by human wisdom, but with words taught by the Spirit, describing spiritual realities in spiritual terms.
>
> Now the natural person does not accept what pertains to the Spirit of God, for to him it is

foolishness, and he cannot understand it, because it is judged spiritually."

God was manifesting his holiness, his intimacy, his covenant commitment, and his love for his people as they journeyed through the desert by this presence of fire.

Another sign of fire is in Exodus13:21,22. It says,

> "The LORD preceded them, in the daytime by means of a column of cloud to show them the way, and at night by means of a column of fire to give them light. Thus they could travel both day and night. Neither the column of cloud by day nor the column of fire by night ever left its place in front of the people."

He is doing the same today in each one of our lives but sometimes unfortunately we fail to see his presence because we are too busy, too unforgiving, too lazy, too arrogant, or too ignorant to take time to be present to him. It is in his presence that the people of Israel were sanctified, and keeping in his presence that we are sanctified today. The Israelites were being sanctified in the desert as they learned obedience and faithfulness. God had to refine – like gold in the fire – all the people he would call his own. Because the Israelites were so contaminated by the ways of the Egyptians God had to refine his people until they understood that he is a holy God and expects his people to be holy.

Stay in His Presence

I have been in churches where holiness and the power of the Holy Spirit are preached and I could actually feel and see the presence of the Holy Spirit manifesting himself among the people. In Exodus 33:11,

> "The LORD used to speak to Moses face to face, as one man speaks to another. Moses would then return to the camp, but his young assistant, Joshua, son of Nun, would not move out of the tent."

I want to be like Joshua and not move out of the presence of his glory - and with good reason. The presence of God's glory was so strong! Moses followed the instructions God gave him to erect the dwelling place and placed the commandments in the innermost court. In Exodus 40:38 it says that,

> "In the daytime the cloud of the LORD was seen over the Dwelling; whereas at night, fire was seen in the cloud by the whole house of Israel in all the stages of their journey."

What were the sins of the Israelites that God was working so hard to remove, before his people could enter the promised land? The main one I believe was idolatry, because idolatry is adultery with God. If we want to experience this kind of glory, we need to take a good look at the ways we are committing idolatry with God. We are a covenant people and we have a covenant with God – meaning we are in a marriage relationship with God. Another sin he was trying to eradicate was the sin of rebellion. Samuel compared rebellion to witchcraft and insubordination to idolatry.

Before we come into God's presence, we need to look at the ways we are rebelling against God and ask God to reveal to whom and where we are being rebellious and insubordinate. Where are the areas in our lives that we rebel against God and his desires for us? Are we rebelling against our husband or wife? Are we rebelling against the responsibilities we have as parents? Are we insubordinate at work, rebelling and complaining about our duties on the job? God hates us to whine and complain in all areas of our lives. Either we do something about the situation or we keep our mouths shut.

We have to stop sinning – stop choosing our will and ways over God's. True happiness comes from being in the center of God's will. It's sad to say that most people are oblivious to sin in their lives because they are not reading the word of God and are not letting the Holy Spirit convict and rid them of their sinfulness. Now is the time to look at the ways we are offending God and ask him to sanctify us. Now! In order to stay in God's presence we need to stay focused on the God who loves us, and serve others as we would serve him.

Oh, that we would see the Holy Spirit fire above all our churches, and places of worship – that we would feel his awesome presence, his glory, and not leave his presence till we were filled with his holiness.

God wants to make us holy and only he can do that. It is the sanctifying grace of the Holy Spirit that we cooperate with which helps us see who we really are in God's sight. Why do we need to be holy? We need to be holy because when we are living a holy, sanctified life, we make it easier for others to find God. They can look at our lives and know that it is possible, and they too can live a normal happy healthy life growing in grace and wisdom. We say that the ministry of the Holy Spirit is to sanctify and make us holy and he will do it if we give him permission and ask for the release of the Baptism of Fire. If you have been baptized for a long time, this grace may have been lying dormant. Now is the time to stir into flame the gifts of wisdom, knowledge, understanding, counsel, piety, and fear of the Lord that God gave us so long ago. How do we do this? By asking the Holy Spirit to come more fully alive in us, to move in power in us and to make us holy. We really have to mean what we say when we pray this prayer because the Spirit knows what is the desire of our heart.

We Should be Ready for Change

When the angel Gabriel told Mary that the Holy Spirit would come upon her and the power of the most high would overshadow her she must have wondered, "Why me?" Only God knew how humble Mary was. He looks for faithfulness and obedience from his children and she had to be the most humble of all. Matthew 1:19 says that Joseph was a righteous man. Of all the people on earth, God chose Mary and Joseph to be examples of this faithfulness and obedience to God. Whenever God said to do something, to leave everyone and everything behind, to pick up and move, and start all over again, they did it. Mary and Joseph had to let go of the opinions of others and do things God's way. This is holiness. They were faithful and obedient. Do you feel sometimes that God is calling you to start all over again, to let go of things and people and pick up and follow him, time and time again? Well, you are probably being sanctified. God wants to know where your heart is. Is it with him first and then others come after God, or do you place yourself or others before him? Our God loves us so passionately and wants us to love him in return. We show our love for him by having an intimate relationship with him and that he comes first in our life.

When the Holy Spirit comes, he empowers us to become all that we can be and to bring light into the darkness of this world. He wants us to walk in his glory. We can not go and baptize all nations without the empowerment of the Holy Spirit. Without the Holy Spirit there would be no life in the church. The Holy Spirit brings life and power, wisdom and knowledge, understanding, counsel and comfort. Let's not waste our lives in worldly pursuits, chasing after things that don't last. It is written in Hebrews 12:1-3,

"Therefore, since we are surrounded by so great a cloud of witnesses, let us rid ourselves of every burden and sin that clings to us and persevere in running the race that lies before us while keeping our eyes fixed on Jesus, the leader and perfecter of faith. For the sake of the joy that lay before him he endured the cross, despising its shame, and has taken his seat at the right of the throne of God. Consider how he endured such opposition from sinners, in order that you may not grow weary and lose heart."

Discipline is Necessary

Our sanctification began 2000 years ago when Jesus took upon himself all our sins, diseases and offenses. He wants to appropriate this grace in us daily. All he needs is our cooperation. He is the deliverer. Further on in Hebrews 12:4-11 we read,

"In your struggle against sin you have not yet resisted to the point of shedding blood. You have also forgotten the exhortation addressed to you as sons:
 'My son, do not disdain the discipline of
  the LORD
 or lose heart when reproved by him;
 for whom the Lord loves, he disciplines,
  he scourges every son he acknowledges.'
Endure your trials as 'discipline'; God treats you as sons. For what 'son' is there whom his father does not discipline? If you are without discipline, in which all have shared, you are not sons but bastards. Besides this, we have had our earthly fathers to discipline us, and we respected them. Should

we not [then] submit all the more to the Father of spirits and live? They disciplined us for a short time as seemed right to them, but he does so for our benefit, in order that we may share his holiness. At the time, all discipline seems a cause not for joy but for pain, yet later it brings the peaceful fruit of righteousness to those who are trained by it."

God allows circumstances in our lives to discipline us, to get our attention, to teach and train us.

The Importance of Our Relationship With God

There was a time in my life that I let myself get so busy and involved in too many things. I have long felt that if Satan can't make you sin, he makes you too busy. I didn't allow myself time with the Lord in prayer, daily scripture reading and staying connected to a believing community. As I slid away from intimacy with God, I became weaker and weaker spiritually. I met and listened to people heavily involved in New Age. I drifted further and further away from God. New Age and all that it involves is idolatry with God and idolatry, as mentioned before, is adultery with God. In any marriage it is important to spend time with your beloved. I didn't take that precious time to talk to and listen to God through prayer, reading, studying scripture, and getting together with a believing community. Many changes were taking place in my life at that time and I became distracted. My God never abandoned me, even though I closed my eyes and ears to his bidding. He loved me enough to keep trying, patiently waiting for me to come back to him. But it took an experience with cancer to bring me to my senses. When I asked God, "Why me?" and took a good hard look at my life, I realized how far I had strayed from the one who loved me the most.

I do not believe God caused my cancer. Some doctors say cancer comes from a combination of factors such as pollution of the air, water or food. Some people blame bad eating habits, or stress, and still others say it's an inability to process grief or maybe just random chance. I'll probably never know what the cause was, but it was a means for my having to quiet down and take a good hard look at my life and how I was choosing to live it. I learned many wonderful lessons by going through this trying time.

First, I learned that when all is said and done we were created out of God's tremendous love for us, that we were made for him and when we die we will spend all eternity enveloped in this enormous love. Or through our laziness, ignorance, arrogance or indifference we chose to spend our life running after other things, and away from God we will lose his love for all eternity.

I learned that perfect love casts out all fear. When I was frightened at the thought of possibly dying and not being present to my family or being in a great deal of pain with the operation I would bring to my remembrance the time I experienced God's love for me. I actually said out loud, "I remember Lord, how you loved me and I know you are loving me right now." I brought to the front of my mind the feelings of love, passion and comfort I experienced years earlier. As I did this, I could feel the fear leaving and his presence getting stronger.

While I was recuperating I had time to think about the ways I had fallen short and I prayed about my relationship with God. As I did I began to realize the many ways I had disappointed God. The strange thing about it was that I never felt judgment or condemnation from God, only a revelation of what I had been doing and that God just wanted me to know so that I could repent and say I was sorry.

Sanctification comes in many different ways and we can learn if only we become sensitive to what God is trying to do.

There's So Much More

Another thing I learned about the sanctification process was that it is very important to stay in the present moment. The past is gone, the future unknown but the present moment is all we have. I learned the importance of paying attention to my thought process, staying in the present moment and just being grateful for that. One day I was driving down the highway and I said to myself, "What are you thinking about?" As I reflected, I began to see how I had been thinking about the past and projecting into the future. Then I focused on the present moment. It was a beautiful sunny day, lovely classical music was on the radio and I was healthy enough to be driving down the road to visit some friends. I began to realize how healthy it is to stop and appreciate each moment thanking God for all his kindness. It is healthy, spiritually, mentally and physically.

I kept praying a prayer, "I trust you Jesus, I trust you Jesus." Now I have learned that Jesus says to me, "I trust you Mary Ellen to care for your body, your soul and your spirit." I found out that it is easier to trust God than to trust myself. I began to understand that Jesus was trusting me to take better care of myself and realized that it is sometimes more difficult to take responsibility for my own well being. As a wife and mother I have spent my life caring for the health of my husband and children. Too often it was easier to think about what others needed, to the exclusion of my own good health. As the Holy Spirit continues to sanctify me, I know now that he also expects me to eat healthier food, exercise each day, get fresh air, and to take time to be with him. He continually shows me the many beautiful and wonderful ways he is revealing his love to me through the beauty of nature and the people he places in my life.

Jesus Gives Us Healing and Freedom

I am now so grateful to be alive. My illness and cure

made me much more grateful to Jesus for what he did for me on Calvary, taking all my sin, shame, blame, guilt and disgrace upon himself, that he could bring it to death with him on the cross. When he resurrected, he brought me back to life with him. He took the just punishment for my fallen sinful nature and it died with him on the cross. It was covered with his blood, which is the holy atonement for my sin and he gave me his eternal life. He paid a terrible price to make me holy. Each day is another day living in his kingdom. I'll be forever grateful. What the enemy meant for my destruction, God uses for his glory and he can do the same for you.

Are you struggling with disappointment, humiliation, loss of a job, divorce, death of a loved one, bad health, financial problems, an alcoholic mate or drug addicted child? God can take your problems and use them for your sanctification. Please don't lose heart. God loves you in the valleys as well as the mountain tops. He is training you to keep your eyes on him. As we go through the crises in life, we learn valuable lessons that are the means of our sanctification if we ask God to teach us what we need to know.

Are there any areas of your life where you have not yet asked for forgiveness? If you have sinned and feel God can't forgive you, please trust me and place yourself and your sinful nature at the foot of the cross. God wants to forgive you and he has a purpose and plan for your good. All you have to do is just tell God you are sorry and promise yourself you'll never do it again. He will strengthen you and give you the grace to let go, but he needs you to come humbly to him.

After I repent of my sin, I picture myself at the foot of the cross and there is a large garbage pail under the feet of Jesus. As I confess my sin I picture myself placing that sin (or sins) into the pail – and then I picture the blood from Jesus hands and feet spilling into the can. When I do this I imagine that my sin evaporates into thin air as the blood touches my sin. God loves to forgive and forget our sins. If you are Catholic, I would also recommend going to confession. The grace from this sacrament lifts your burdens better than any medicine can.

St. Paul encouraged the Hebrews in chapter 12:12-14 when he said,

> "So strengthen your drooping hands and your weak knees. Make straight paths for your feet, that what is lame may not be dislocated but healed.
> Strive for peace with everyone, and for that holiness without which no one will see the Lord."

Yearn for Sanctification

Holiness doesn't mean we've always been good and stayed out of trouble, or always will. Holiness is founded on true humility and the ability to say, "I'm sorry, Lord," and knowing that Jesus took all – our every thought, word and deed - to the cross with him so that we could be free to walk as a child of God. It was not because of some good we have done, but because of the great love Jesus has for us. He did it for us on Calvary. 1 Corinthians 3:16 says,

> "Do you not know that you are the temple of God, and that the Spirit of God dwells in you?"

It is God's presence in us that makes us holy. We are only weak human beings, who are walking tabernacles containing a holy God. He is our strength, courage and power. When we need any virtue, whether it is to love more, to forgive, to be patient or what ever, we can ask the Holy Spirit within, to move in this virtue in us. I have tried it many times and it works. St. Paul warns the Corinthians, in 1 Corinthians 4:18-20,

"Some have become inflated with pride, as if I were not coming to you. But I will come to you soon, if the Lord is willing, and I shall ascertain not the talk of these inflated people but their power. For the kingdom of God in not a matter of talk but of POWER" (emphasis added).

This power is the presence of God in us and comes from intimacy with God. It is God's presence in us and it comes from our daily walk with him. You can observe people who have intimacy with God by their fruits of love, peace and joy.

Thanksgiving and Praise Brings Us Into God's Presence

When I attend prayer meetings that are extremely powerful in praise, worship, adoration, tongues, interpretation of tongues, sharing the word of God and sharing what God has done in their lives that week, I know immediately that the people present in the room have been reading their scriptures during the week and having time alone with God in prayer each day. They are filled with God's presence and when they come to a prayer meeting they are ready to share what God has been doing in their lives because they have been watching what God was doing, and listening to God all week.

On the other hand, I have also gone to some prayer meetings that are more of a songfest and social hour than a charismatic prayer meeting. These people have the gifts, but are not using them daily nor having intimacy with God during the week in prayer and scripture reading. They can not share anything important, because they spent too little time with God and are not keeping alert to what he is trying to do in their lives.

If we are to have healthy prayer meetings and revival in our church, we need to understand the importance of thanksgiving and praise. "I will enter his gates with thanksgiving in my heart, I will enter his courts with praise," is a song we sing. Unfortunately, we stop there. When we look at the structure of the house of God that Moses taught the Israelites to build, we see that there were three parts to the worship space. They were: the outer court; the inner court; and the innermost court which was the most sacred space where the high priest could enter only once a year to make atonement for the sins of the people. This innermost court was also called the Holy of Holies and it was where the Ark of the Covenant rested. It was the most sacred place where the presence of God resided. The flame (representing God's presence) could be seen over it at night.

When we enter through the gate with thanksgiving- we reach the outer court. Then we keep going into the inner court with our worship or praise, but unfortunately we settle for staying in the inner court with our worship, and then leave satisfied that we have done something good - we thanked and worshipped God. It is however in the inner most court that the presence and glory of God is the strongest.

Matthew 27:51 says, that as Jesus died and gave up his spirit,

> "And behold, the veil of the sanctuary was torn in two from top to bottom."

What was the significance of the veil, of the Holy of Holies, ripping it in two from top to bottom? It meant that because of Jesus and what he did for us on Calvary, God (from the top) gave us access and permission to enter into the Holy of Holies. Jesus made a way for us to enter into his Glory, signified by the Holy of Holies – the innermost court.

Yet we seldom if ever, enter this holy place where the presence of God is so strong. We stay either by the gate of the outer court thanking God, or in the inner court, worshipping. Are you asking, "So how do we arrive in the innermost court – this Holy of Holies?" The answer is by continuing to praise and worship God in all situations – both good and bad. That is the power that keeps you moving right into the presence of God.

Many years ago we moved to Miami from New York, where all my family and friends lived. I didn't know anyone in Miami and found myself very lonely caring for four young children. I met a wonderful woman who I greatly admired and she called me on the phone. Even though we talked for a while I did not share my feelings of loneliness and isolation. Another week went by and these feelings turned into depression. When she called me again I still did not confide in her and pretended everything was fine, until she said to me, "Mary Ellen, God loves you." I wanted to scream! I said to her, "Pam, you don't know what I am feeling right now. I don't feel love, I can't love, and I don't want to think about love."

That's when Pam taught me one of the most important lessons in my life. She questioned me and said, "When you light a match in a dark room what happens?" I told her, "the room gets brighter." She said, "That's right, the darkness can't stay where there is light." She reminded me that God inhabits the praise of his people and wherever people are praising him, his light comes with him. "When you get off the phone, Mary Ellen, I want you to do two things. First, thank him for this situation, just as it is. And the second is to sing a joyful happy song of praise to him – just as you are." I could hardly hold back the tears as I said to her, "I don't think I can. I'd be a hypocrite. I really don't feel that way." She encouraged me again and when I finished the phone call I figured that I had nothing to lose if I did what she said.

As I wiped the kitchen counter I told God, "I don't know why I am thanking you for this situation but Pam says to do it, so I am. Thank you God for the feelings I have, just as they are. Thank you that you love me even now. Thank you that I don't have to be perfect to receive your love." Then, I began to thank him for having a roof over my head, food on my table, that my children were all healthy, that it was a sunny day. As I tried to sing, "The Joy of the Lord is My Strength," tears spilled into my sink. However, within about ten minutes of thanking and praising God, I began to feel the depression lifting. Periodically during the day, as I felt the negative feeling returning, I resumed the thanksgiving and worship. I did this for two days and what took two weeks to develop vanished completely. I had learned how important thanksgiving and praise was to bring in the presence of God.

Now, many years later, I've learned that as I continue to praise and worship for some time the presence of God gets stronger and stronger. I want to encourage you to keep going – take the time to continue to praise and worship in songs and prayers. God passionately yearns to love us and when we enter the holy place we come to a place where we allow God to flow around us, in us and through us. He regenerates us.

When you enter the glory of God, the Holy Spirit will take over and reveal himself to you in very powerful ways, first of all in revealing His love to you, and then by healing and delivering you. Oh! When you taste his glory you will never be the same again. He is moving very powerfully now in revival glory. I challenge you to taste of his glory and tell me that you are not changed dramatically. He is pouring out his oil of gladness and wants us to come to him for it.

Like the ten virgins with their lanterns – I want to be in the group of five that have their lanterns full with a supply of oil to last me through the night. That oil comes from the Holy Spirit and is ours for the asking. I encourage you to ask for your supply. It is the oil of gladness, so that we may be ready for when the bridegroom arrives.

The work of the Holy Spirit is to sanctify us so that we too may be a holy people. That's probably why his symbol is fire. We are on a journey with God and his refining fire is at work in us just as it was with the Israelites. We can not make ourselves holy by doing, or not doing specific things. But we can open ourselves to the Holy Spirit, and present ourselves as we are, with all our weaknesses, our sins, and offenses, and ask him to make us holy so that we may experience his glory and his presence more concretely.

CHAPTER ELEVEN

Ask for More

We all want to leave behind a legacy to our loved ones. While some think of money and possessions as an appropriate inheritance, the greatest gift I want to pass on to my loved ones is the gift of appreciating the Holy Spirit because he is Jesus' gift to us, his church.

When my loved ones understand why Jesus came, and have a revelation of who he is, and what he did for them on Calvary, they will want him to be their Lord and Savior, the source of all love. They can let go of the opinions of others and live for God's opinion of them.

When they ask for the release of the power of the Holy Spirit and receive his ministerial gifts they will be able to accomplish the purpose and plan God has for them. They will also be able to worship him the way he wants to be worshipped – in Spirit and truth.

As they are being faithful and obedient to his will for them in their lives, his sanctifying grace will produce the fruits of the Holy Spirit mentioned in Galatians 5:22,23.

"The fruit of the Spirit is love, joy, peace, patience, kindness, generosity, faithfulness, gentleness, self-control."

They can walk in the glory and love of God, sensing his presence, his love, joy, peace, etc. Isaiah 11:2,3 says that,

"The spirit of the LORD shall rest upon him:
a spirit of wisdom and of understanding,
A spirit of counsel and of strength,
a spirit of knowledge and of fear of the LORD,
and his delight shall be the fear of the LORD."

These are the sanctifying gifts of the Holy Spirit and I trust the Spirit to manifest himself in them to sanctify and make them holy. By the way, the gift of the fear of the Lord means to have an awesome respect of God and comes with a promise. Psalm 112:1-4 tells us,

"Happy are those who fear the LORD,
who greatly delight in God's commands.
Their descendants shall be mighty in the land,
a generation upright and blessed.
Wealth and riches shall be in their homes;
their prosperity shall endure forever.
They shine through the darkness, a light for the upright;
they are gracious, merciful, and just."

And the list goes on, but you can see there are rewards for those, and their loved ones, who love God and treat him with respect. Love is the most important ingredient – the Father's divine love for us in creating us and in sending Jesus as the atonement for our sins. Then our love for God in letting him love us as he wants to, recognizing his love all around us during the day and allowing his Spirit freedom to worship in us and empower us to become all he knows we can become.

More than anything, I want my loved ones to know that there is a big difference between human love and divine love. I believe that if they understand the three elements of Matthew 3:11 and implement them in their lives, they will be able to allow the free flow of the Holy Spirit who is the Divine Love to move in and through them. When they feel they are incapable of loving someone I hope they will come to know that the Divine Lover is within. He can and will love through them. Whatever virtue they need is already in them. God is all virtue and when we live in God and he lives in us, all we have to do is to call on him and allow his presence to move through us. Jesus is Lord and wants to be lord in our lives, but we have to ask him to move through us. If we need to love, forgive, be more patient, be less critical, etc. we need to ask him to be lord of this void in our life. I used to ask for patience, but now I just say to God, "You are all virtue in me, please take over and be Lord. Let your patience flow through me." And within a few minutes his peace is flowing in me.

1 John 4:7-13 says it best.

> "Beloved, let us love one another, because love is of God; everyone who loves is begotten by God and knows God. Whoever is without love does not know God, for God is love. In this way the love of God was revealed to us: God sent his only Son into the world so that we might have life through him. In this is love: not that we have loved God, but that he loved us and sent his Son as expiation for our sins. Beloved, if God so loved us, we also must love one another. No one has ever seen

God. Yet, if we love one another, God remains in us, and his love is brought to perfection in us.

This is how we know that we remain in him and he in us, that he has given us of his Spirit."

Such a simple sentence, "This is how we know that we remain in him and he in us, that he has given us of his Spirit." With the power of the Holy Spirit in us, we can do and become all things. The rest of this scripture says,

"Moreover, we have seen and testify that the Father sent his Son as savior of the world. Whoever acknowledges that Jesus is the Son of God, God remains in him and he in God. We have come to know and to believe in the love God has for us.

God is love, and whoever remains in love remains in God and God in him. In this is love brought to perfection among us, that we have confidence on the day of judgment because as he is, so are we in this world. There is no fear in love, but perfect love drives out fear because fear has to do with punishment, and so one who fears is not yet perfect in love. We love because he first loved us."
(1John 4:14-19)

Our God is a God of love. First He loves us. As we call to him and hunger for more of him we begin to recognize his presence in our life and that he was, and is already loving us. A friend of mine said we should pray for a revelation – a revelation of God – which is to know and to understand who God is. God wants to reveal himself to us but he is a gentleman and will not impose himself on us. He needs to be invited into our lives and when we do invite him he comes with so much love and gentleness words cannot express the experience.

In 1 Peter 1:13-16 it says,

> "Therefore, gird up the loins of your mind, live soberly, and set your hopes completely on the grace to be brought to you at the revelation of Jesus Christ. Like obedient children, do not act in compliance with the desires of your former ignorance but, as he who called you is holy, be holy yourselves in every aspect of your conduct, for it is written, 'Be holy because I [am] holy.'"

This would be an impossible task if it were not for the death and resurrection of Jesus being appropriated in our lives. God does not expect you to do more than is humanly possible, but he wants and expects us to take responsibility for coming to him for the help we need, so that he may empower us with his Holy Spirit, who will do it in us if we allow him.

I have found out that there is a big difference between human love and divine love and that there is so much more of God's glory and goodness. I want it all and especially for those I love.

I heard a wonderful story told by the late Fr. Harold Cohen, SJ at a conference. He said he was a quiet child and hadn't learned to speak yet. One day while his mother was feeding him, she took the spoon out of his mouth and before she could get the food back onto his spoon, he said with such urgency, "More, more. I want more." He said his mother was stunned, since he had never spoken a word before this. Father Hal encouraged us to say to the Holy Spirit, "I want more, Holy Spirit, more of you!" And I say it to you. Hunger for more of the Holy Spirit. Ask for more. Your life will be richer for it.

In Matthew 9:37,38 Jesus told his disciples,

"The harvest is abundant but the laborers are few; so ask the master of the harvest to send out laborers for his harvest."

We are the laborers. God's people are so hungry and so ready to hear the word of God. I see it especially in the young people. When we give Life in the Spirit seminars to the students preparing for Confirmation at first they are reticent but after they hear about real life experiences they come alive and begin to open their minds and hearts to the Holy Spirit. There is a beautiful hymn called,
"Bringing in the Sheaves," which tells about harvesting the crop. I pray that when I stand before God and he says, "What did you collect?" he'll look behind me and see several 18-wheeler trucks packed with the sheaves.

God does not send us into the fields without tools or farm equipment. He supplies the equipment in the form of his gifts mentioned in 1 Corinthians 12. It's time to go out there and bring in the crop. We don't have an option. We have an assignment. Bring in the crop, the harvest is ripe!

We can only do this with the help of the Holy Spirit. So ask the Holy Spirit for more of himself in your life – he will be your power! He can and will transform your life if you let him. He wants to reveal the Father's love to you. He wants to reveal Jesus to you. He wants to set your captive spirit free. He wants to bring healing, wholeness, and deliverance into your life so that you may be free to stand in his glory and receive his love for you more fully. He has so much more to give you. My prayer for my loved ones and you is that you will say, "Yes" as Mary did. Say "Yes, Holy Spirit I want more of you – Come Holy Spirit and release more of you in me. I want you more than anything."